Translating
the Queer

T0314855

About the author

Héctor Domínguez Ruvalcaba is a professor in the Department of Spanish and Portuguese at the University of Texas, Austin, where he teaches queer and gender issues in Latin American literature, film, and culture.

Translating the Queer

Body Politics and Transnational Conversations

Héctor Domínguez Ruvalcaba

ZED
Zed Books
London

Translating the Queer: Body Politics and Transnational Conversations
was first published in 2016 by Zed Books Ltd, The Foundry,
17 Oval Way, London SE11 5RR, UK.

www.zedbooks.net

Typeset in Adobe Garamond by Swales & Willis Ltd, Exeter, Devon
Index by Rohan Bolton
Cover design by Andrew Brash

A catalogue record for this book is available from the British Library.

ISBN 978-1-78360-293-3 hb
ISBN 978-1-78360-292-6 pb
ISBN 978-1-78360-294-0 pdf
ISBN 978-1-78360–295-7 epub
ISBN 978-1-78360-296-4 mobi

Contents

Acknowledgments

I am very thankful for the help of my readers—Carlos Amador, Adam Coon, Ruth Rubio, and Nat Zingg—who were generous with their time and meticulous in every paragraph. I also appreciate the suggestions and comments of the anonymous reviewers and the patience and professionalism of the Zed Books editor Kika Sroka-Miller.

This book has been the result of a long journey of conferences, symposia, edited books, political activism, and formal and informal conversations with most of the authors referenced. In this sense, this book can be considered a summary of transnational dialogues with a rich critical mass and relentless activists. The Sexualities Section of the Latin American Studies Association, the international series of conferences Queering Paradigms, and the Permanent Seminar on Gender Violence, among other meetings around the Americas, have been of vital importance in writing this volume. I cannot mention all the great people I have interacted with in the past years, but their inspiration, passion, and good sense of community are all present in these pages.

I want to especially thank the following writers, academics, artists, and activists, who kindly agreed to be interviewed: Pedro Lemebel, Juan Pablo Sutherland, Gloria Thiers, Carmen Berenguer, Gloria Careaga, Alejandro Brito, César Enríquez Cabaret, Violeta Barrientos, Sara Rondinel, Óscar Vega, Rosario Aquim, Elvira Espejo, Daniel Jones, Esteban Paulón, Osvaldo Bazán, Camilo

Antillón, and Milú Vargas. Their work in politics, research, art, and journalism has been influential in the recent history of gender and sexuality in Latin America, and I'm very fortunate for having had the opportunity to talk personally to all of them, as many of their ideas are central to this project.

Introduction: Troubles and travels of the queer

What is the place of queerness in Latin American culture and politics? How did it become an object of academic, artistic, and intellectual conversations? What meanings does queer acquire in its translation into Latin American cultural codes? This is a study of the queer as a field located in a specific geography and culture, not as a universal notion. *Translating the Queer* takes the Latin American region and its cultural diaspora as a territory of political action and conversation on issues related to transgressive sexualities and body conceptions. The field of queer in Latin America includes political actions, academic agendas, artistic movements, and economic development. Additionally, the queer noun and adjective can be applied to policies, movements, fields of representation, aesthetic practices, and moral debates. Latin America as a geographic demarcation of queer involves a complex cultural dynamic in which bodies have conducted and been transformed by practices, meanings, and policies of sexuality that occur inherently to the historical processes of the region.

How gender, sexuality, and the politics of the body have been approached in Latin America in recent academic and political debates is the main focus of this work. That is, this book addresses how queer criticism and theory have contributed to Latin Americanist scholarship and how the theory has transcended the field of sex and gender studies. As we will see, the field of queer studies is specific as it focuses on the cultural implications of sexuality and the body, but it is also extensive, as it intervenes in and affects cultural processes in general. Politics, norms, tastes, economy, and language are embodied, gendered, and sexualized. My focus is to understand how this politics, semantics, aesthetics, and ethics of sex and bodies has become one of the most transgressive meaning producers in contemporary Latin American culture.

In this book, it is my ambition to offer an inquiry into how queer phenomena have been represented and defined, and how they have constituted a set of cultural and political practices. Those deviant bodily practices were there, *avant la lettre*, before queer theory came to academia. Queer academic discourse, as well as political and artistic movements, constructed a corpus of representations, actions, and methodologies to illuminate obscured and denied aspects of cultural history, a rewriting of history that tends to go beyond the mere academic exercise. In this book, queer is a form of understanding the politics of the body. This implies a criticism of the hegemonic culture, the legal system, and the gender structure. Queering is an understanding of the deviant as a subject of historical change in the cultural and political realms. This is a study of the troubles and contentions that take place in representations and debates on body, sex, and gender in contemporary Latin America. I chose the focus of the contention and troubles in consonance with the notion of queer as the point of destabilization, the fissure through which the order is challenged, and the point of fracture of what is considered natural, normal, or legitimate about body, sex, and gender.

Queering is a process of resignification of the conceptions and norms that control the body in Latin American culture. The distinctive conception and practice of the queer in the region will be the main object of this inquiry. What, then, are the specifics of a region that necessarily relocates the notion of queer? We can summarize, somewhat arbitrarily, the Latin American queer conversation in the following statements: a) Latin American queer studies have been undertaken in a transnational dialogue, which implies a politics of cultural translation; b) colonialism/decolonization is a tension implicit in the articulation of queer dissidences; c) queerness has been associated with modernity in most twentieth-century debates on gender and sexuality; d) queer is a methodology of critical thinking that by deconstructing the gender system questions the foundations of the nation and the state; and e) the machineries of consumption and disposability of neoliberalism complicate the processes of body liberation and queer expressions.

Latin American queer studies have been undertaken in a transnational dialogue, which implies a politics of cultural translation

My primary corpus of analysis is the scholarship produced in the past three decades by academics and intellectuals writing both from within Latin America and from abroad. This inside–outside crossing describes a number of contacts, influences, and contradictions that define the queer as a conjuncture that propels a crisis of the gender system. Latin American sex–gender culture and politics is an entity constructed from various cartographies and from multiple discursive and theoretical traditions. The travel of queer concepts and representational practices through the gay and lesbian research approaches, or through feminism, psychoanalysis, and sexology, has produced a rich corpus of cultural and political translation.

Far from undertaking a process of acculturation by transplanting cultural systems and metropolitan theories, Latin Americanist queer scholars and creators translocate discourses and cultural practices between radical Western debates and the troubled realities of the queer Latin American population. This is not a simple movement from the center to the periphery in a paternalistic gesture, but rather a collaborative exchange of ideas, politics, and representations. In her introduction to the anthology *Translocalities/Translocalidades: Feminist Politics of Translation in the Latin/a Américas*, Sonia Alvarez (2014) explains the cultural dynamics that characterizes Latin American translocality: "[r]ather than immigrating and 'assimilating,' ... many people in the Latin/a Américas increasingly move back and forth between localities, between historically situated and culturally specific (though increasingly porous) places, across multiple borders, and not just between nations" (2). In fact, many people from the south travel, write, and teach in the north and vice versa. Many people from the south work and teach in the south but maintain a dialogue with their northern counterparts. In fact, the great majority of authors and artists referenced in this book navigate within these transnational, translinguistic, transepistemological channels.

This border crossing, this transmigration of discursive practices, performs a politics of translation. Translation is a form of mediation that, as in the cases of feminist or queer discourses, deals not only with the logic that would communicate the semantics of the translated text but also with rhetoric, that untranslatable part that according to Gayatri C. Spivak is not expressed in the logic of language but in its disruption, the poetic fissure of language where the affect is performed. It is in this rhetoricity where we can find an alterity implied in the language, as a meaningful silence that demands an affective equivalence in the target language (Spivak 2012: 181). "The relationship between logic and rhetoric, between grammar and rhetoric, is also a relationship between social logic, social reasonableness, and the disruptiveness of figuration in social practice" (186–187). Is it then impossible to translate the silence of disruption, the resistance to the logic of reason, to the naturalized forms of oppression? Is then queerness untranslatable?

If we expect translation to reproduce the totality of the semantics and affective uses of the original text, then we believe that translation must be loyal to the seminal language system, rather than letting the discourse travel and undertake the adventure of discovering—or creating—a new set of meaning according to the politics of the translation itself. Rigid loyalty to the original in the translated version was, in effect, the intentionality of the translation of the doctrines and precepts that constituted the colonial discourse. What is lost in translation is untranslatable (Lavinas and Viteri 2016: 4). The politics of translation that disavows loyalty is rather concerned with the need of the discourse to be a liberating impulse from the precepts of the colonial—that is, a decolonizing translation. This politics of translation works for the formation of a new discourse in the travel destiny of the queer text. Rather than being focused on preserving its original stage (its social contexts, its cultural features, its political use staged in the drama of origin of the discourse), it is a rewritten discourse, as the social stage and culture into which the queer text is translated presents different challenges from those of the context from which it emerged. They are discourses that come to deal with other contexts where sexual dissidents and gender-nonconforming subjects demand an appropriation of queer knowledge's liberating character.

Queer theory in Latin America is a method through which local troubles can be viewed. Its meaning is enriched through a complex intersectionality in which sexuality and gender expressions cannot be detached from economic determinants; religious and legal constraints; racial, class, and nationality exclusions; or political conjunctures. The translation of queer, then, is a political process that involves the recognition of the margins, exclusions, abjections, and oppressions of alternative bodies. In her introduction to the volume *Gender in Translation*, Sherry Simon (1996) proposes that, in the translation of gender texts, it is most important to make clear the effects and responses of the translated text in the target language (7). This question allows us to understand translation of queer texts as a political action that contributes to changes in knowledge and practices of the body. How has this translation of theory become a politics in the sex–gender system in Latin American culture? How is power manifested in the act of transporting meaning, or remaking it in the unavoidable paraphrasing that translation undertakes? Simon's proposal of translating gender texts in order to elicit a response suggests queer text translation will also have a politics implied in the translation itself.

Nonetheless, this queer politics of translation does not begin with the actual translation into a second language. Before queer is translated, it has already exercised a political effect in the field of identity categories, politics, and knowledge of the body. Annamarie Jagose (1996) observes that the AIDS pandemic has been a determinant for reconsidering categories of identification, power, and knowledge: this process coincides with what queer theory does with respect to the sex–gender hegemony (94). Questioning constituted identities and enabling the emergence of new ones originating in the abjected and the excluded is the political action that queer theory performs, according to Jagose's definition. I argue that, beyond the actual translation, the effect of queer discourse in Latin America is the rearticulation of the social and political meaning of the body, a disrupting reordering of the gender system. In her analysis of the immigrant and ethnic literature in the United States as a translating phenomenon, Martha J. Cutter (2005) underlines the semantic findings undertaken in cultural translation that enrich and subvert the hegemonic discourse itself by conglomerating a variety of meaning systems (60). In the same sense, translating queer politics and culture is itself a work that disrupts codifications and threatens the order of meanings that provides coherence to a culture. It is my purpose to analyze those troubling points in which the intervention of queer theory and representation opens the way to reconsidering norms, definitions, tastes, and culture. In other words, my discussion will follow the main political, intellectual, and academic conversations that have been in place since LGBT culture and politics, and queer theory, arrived in Latin America.[1]

Ethnography, literature, and other forms of representation have produced a field of knowledge of the nonhegemonic body, its politics, its aesthetics, and its ethos. When the word *queer* traveled, the trauma of its discriminatory origin stayed at home. It came dressed as a field of study, a political position, an aesthetic proposal, and a lifestyle. In all these actions, representations, and approaches, works dealing with queer issues have been focused on traumas, conflicts, and alternative subjectivities located in Latin American societies.

It is not the intention of this book to debate about what is the correct translation of *queer*. As a bordering concept, it cannot be measured under any prescribing discourse (that would be a colonialist view of translation). The place of queer, according to Mexican American intellectual Gloria Anzaldúa (1999), is located in between, is permanently in transit, a continuous escaping from the boundaries of meaning (71). That movement is inherent to both queerness and translation, as the *trans* morpheme describes a displacement, the former from the hegemonic gender system and the latter from one system of meanings to another. It is a poetics of normalcy disruption. I call it poetics because its discursive nature of breaking the logic of the binary social order is effective in both

---

[1] While I agree with Brad Epps when he pinpoints the impossibilities of translating *queer* into Spanish, as it loses its pejorative connotations that make it an emotionally loaded word in English, I also have to recognize that the concepts, images, methods, and lexicon associated with *queer* have been useful in unveiling practices, representations, fears, and desires and in constituting alternative identities (Epps 2008: 897–898).

the field of meaning and the field of the body. If the queer body experiences the in-between rhetoric, it is itself an entity, or a subject, in a state of translation. The coincidence of the transnational/ translocated site of conversation where queer Latin American studies occur, the theoretical task of translating as politics, and the in-between position of the queer subject confirm the liminality of queer studies. While I recognize that many nuances and much affective content of the concepts and images are lost in translation, I find it more productive to build on what is found in translation than to regret what is missed in that process.

Colonialism/decolonization is a tension implicit in the articulation of queer dissidences

Instead of talking about another liberating utopia—replacing the lesbian and gay agendas—what queer theory does, at least in the Latin American cultural contexts, has the effect of unveiling a variety of forms of disidentification that are in place as the invisible threads of sexual colonialism. Cuban American critic José Esteban Muñoz (1999) bases the idea of disidentification on his analysis of queer-of-color performance in the United States, which he deems nonconfrontational but also differentiated from the hegemonic gender–race structures through rhetorical strategies that enable the emergence of what he calls "identities-in-difference," which refers to the rejection of the stereotype imposed by others where this rejection is expressed by appropriating such stigmatization in order to positively resignify it. Identity-in-difference stages a failure in socially imposed identity. In the case of queer people of color in the United States, it is clear that, while they are identified by the dominant ideology of the mainstream of racial and sexual differences, those interpellations are stereotypically negative, and consequently these people do not receive the privileges of white gays and lesbians. Their difference is sexual and racial, adding an intersectional aspect that complicates their identity formation (that condition would also question the need of the ontological question that asks about identity: *Who am I?*).

The mediating position of the Latin American colonized queer is not only aimed at the construction of a hybrid species of the field of dissident sexualities but also it seeks the deconstruction of the very notion of identity, undermining its exclusionary character and tendency to territoriality. By opening the rooms of identity, contaminating their defining features, and trespassing on their borders, rather than enacting a harmonious assembly, disidentification politics can be described as a battleground of meaning, as cultural turmoil that happens in the representations and theories of the colonized queer. As a place of encounter, collapse, and a continuous state of conflict, sex–gender meanings and practices are constantly redefined, forbidden, and sublimated. As American historian Michael J. Horswell (2005) observes in his *Decolonizing the Sodomite*, colonization reduced to the concept of sodomy all sex practices outside Catholic sanctions (15). This epistemological violence had the effect of dislocating a more fluid conception of gender and sex, of complicating even more those practices that were already problematic in pre-Columbian cultures. In the process of transculturation, I argue, colonizers and colonized people negotiated the rules of sex behavior and the place of identities. Although it is an asymmetric relationship, and the sexuality of the colonized became an object of scrutiny and surveillance, other factors beyond the judiciary system of the church enabled the clandestine practices of nonlegitimate sex. This silenced and denied zone of Latin American sexuality, with all its intersectionalities with race and class, has been the focus of attention in what we can call Latin Americanist queer scholarship.

If being a transnational conversation is one of the most remarkable characteristics of Latin American queer studies, does this fact signify a new theoretical colonialism and then another wave of colonized knowledge? That has been one of the most common criticisms of queer studies in some forums in recent years. The transnational and exogenous place of enunciation of the theory—very often written in US and European university centers, following the route of previous colonizing discourses—seems to be the main reason for perceiving queer studies as another colonialist intervention. Indeed, colonialism establishes a circuit of enunciation and translation that assigns the Latin American subject the role of a receptor of knowledge produced and authenticated in the hegemonic centers of meaning production—what Antonio Gramsci (1971) called the hegemonic apparatus. This binomial reduction of the colonial relationship hinders the possibility of valuing important efforts of liberating the subaltern queer body from the oppressive system in metropolitan societies. In fact, several academic studies produced in the northern hemisphere are decolonizing as they are concerned with sex–gender–race–class intersectionality of subaltern populations. Gloria Anzaldúa (1999, 2002, 2002b, 2015), Cherrí Moraga (1983), José Esteban Muñoz (1999, 2009), among other US Latino/a scholars, understand queer as the uncomfortable place in between, the no-place, or the place of disidentification, in which queer migrants and queer people of color find their place. It is precisely this unstable space that the colonized occupy as the site of their subjectification. That is, becoming a citizen with full rights depends on the way one's identity is rearticulated in order to make feasible a project of citizenship construction that is not violent against the queer and racialized body. This means not going anywhere outside the postcolonial, neocolonial, and colonial power relationships that characterize Latin American societies and instead acting from the inside of this colonizing political system. Queer Latin American theory, like many other aspects of cultural and knowledge production, is articulated inside coloniality; many of its concepts and arguments have even been articulated within the centers of power and written in the language of empire. Nonetheless, this queer-of-color production represents the uncanny side of the imperial corpus of knowledge. It constitutes the dissident side of the metropolis. Queer expressions are cornered in the realm of the abject for both colonizing and colonized cultures. They are the area of the borderland, the place of the *atravesados*: "*Los atravesados* live here; the squint-eyed, the perverse, the queer, the troublesome, the mongrel, the mulatto, the half-breed, the half-dead; in short, those who cross over, pass over, or go through the confines of the 'normal'" (Anzaldúa 1999: 25). This place of the abject described by Anzaldúa is the place of the borderlander, which is relatively undetermined—a geography that divides colonized from colonizer countries. Rather, the cartography of the abject—those excluded from the normal—inhabit the outsides of privileges, being racialized, gendered, or sexualized, regardless of the actual geographic location of this outside. Rosamond S. King (2014) defines the subject of queer criticism as translocal. Translocals are the transmigrants who inhabit the peripheral circuits of extreme capitalism, the last stance of colonialism. King observes that the place of the translocated is a privileged one, both in terms of being an agent of globalization of the local knowledges and in terms of functioning as a translator between the metropolis and peripheral colonized cultures. The risks of this mediation are intrinsic to the political and cultural challenges of this process of traveling meanings.

Queerness has been associated with modernity in most twentieth-century debates on gender and sexuality

In this process of translation, visualizing diverse sexualities functions as a contentious inscription of alternative forms of life in the national imaginaries, especially for the anticolonial tendency of liberal discourses that dominate Latin American intellectual and academic spaces. Queer cannot be translated into a rational logic of the culture and gender system but is estranged from it. Queer culture and discourse have already emerged as the other's tongue in their culture of origin. They had to be translated into the hegemonic discourse of metropolitan academia. Now, queer has come to be translated into another cultural system, which already has its own contradictions and political dynamics. I argue this translation of queer occurs as a countercultural intervention into the culture in which it arrives as a translated concept. But this intervention does not come without controversy: as a theory coming from the so-called global north, queerness has been under suspicion of being another expression of colonialism, as it is considered a distinctive mark of modernity. Nevertheless, it is arguable that queerness is, in fact, an instrument of decolonization, in which translation plays a key role as a linguistic process where meaning is put into crisis.

Colonial anxiety contextualizes several phenomena: the arrival of queer modernity in the period of *modernismo* (a Hispanic aesthetic movement that arose at the turn of the twentieth century); the controversies of revolutionaries and queer intellectuals in Mexico and Cuba; the military persecution of sexual dissidents (deemed antinational bodies) in the Southern Cone's Dirty War; and even the sexual tourism and human trafficking of the neoliberal system. These are some instances in which queer thought and representations have gone and still go through multiple processes of resistance that end up constituting alternative identities and undertaking a politics of recognition, of liberation, and of the establishment of rights. Moreover, queer modernization foments an economy and a wide range of aesthetic expressions and forms of social participation. This troubling moment of cultural translation of liberating discourses on gender and sexuality and their contestations in Latin American culture contextualized the emergence of alternative identities that would be recognized as modern.

The modern history of sexual dissidence departs, then, from the state's strategies of exclusion and advances toward inclusion of gender and sexual dissidence within citizenship. In this process, we can observe the constitution of queer modern myths: queer is the avant-garde of modernization; queer represents foreign and colonialist influences; an important sector of creative and intellectual elite places the queer topic in the public scene as part of cosmopolitan and universal culture; and queer politics, like feminism, places the body on the agenda of public concerns and constitutes one of the largest civil movements of our time. This meaning formation of the queer as an expression of modernity describes a traveling culture that takes the route of modern Western civilization, the route of sexual knowledge, as described by Foucault (1990) in his *History of Sexuality*: from its status of nefarious sin to criminalization, medicalization, and finally a politics of identity and of inclusion in citizenship. For the historiographical works discussing the incorporation of the queer into the national imaginaries, this narrative of modernization as the incorporation of sexual dissidence transgresses the traditional gender structure, identified as Catholic and patriarchal, and advances toward the paradise of freedom, where nonhegemonic desires finally enjoy legitimacy. Both colonial and liberation agendas coincide in this queer modernity. In this sense, LGBT activism came from metropolitan countries as a liberation movement; it is part of the paradoxes of the postcolonial condition. The movement's exogenous character has been one of the main points of rejection from nationalistic discourses, such as the revolutionary ideology in Mexico and Cuba and in Southern Cone twentieth-century dictatorships. It seems like the main struggle queer modernity has to face is this rejection from the national identity, which leads to one of the main subjects of conversation in queer Latin Americanist scholarship.

Queer is a methodology of critical thinking that by deconstructing the gender system questions the foundations of the nation and the state

Inscribing the queer in the national community is one of the main topics we find in a series of national histories of nonhegemonic sexualities: Emilio Bejel's *Gay Cuban Nation* (2001), Osvaldo Bazán's *Historia de la homosexualidad en Argentina* (2004), and James Green's *Beyond Carnival* (1999), to name a few of the most representative monographs. Historiography provides evidence of a proscribed bodily culture. It is a form of writing whose main endeavor is the compilation of stories, images, places, practices, and symbols that pertain to underground excluded communities. To depict the life of the excluded is to expose those images and sexual practices that have been covered, denied, and punished. They make visible what is considered obscene (i.e., what is not proper to be shown in public). The politics of the history of sexual diversity is to incorporate the marginalized sexuality into the realm of citizenship. Then, queer historiography proposes a reconfiguration of the national subject, overcoming the patriarchal and heterosexual basis of the modern liberal state.

This inscription places the queer subject as a symptom of the modernization of Latin American culture. I use the word *symptom* on purpose to underline medicalization as one of the mechanisms of exclusion and control of sexual dissidence undertaken by modern institutions. The second strategy of exclusion and control of sexual dissidence is criminalization. When homoeroticism becomes an illness to be treated and a vice to be corrected, it stops being an unspeakable practice and instead becomes a topic of body knowledge. The first approaches to sexual differences were the medical and criminalist treatises written in the late nineteenth and early twentieth centuries. These scientific works aimed toward the establishment of public policies regarding sexual and gender dissidence and are now one of the main materials used by historians of homosexuality in Latin America. This disciplinary archive offers a unique compendium of bodily accounts that allows historians to understand how subjects were excluded, the mechanisms of exclusion, and the formation of cultural imaginaries that would provide elements for the remaking of national demarcations and inclusions.

The nationalization of the queer is a trope we can find performed in a substantial number of artistic projects all around the continent. In 1994 the Chilean artist Juan Dávila triggered one of the most significant controversies regarding nationalism and queerness with his painting of a transvestite Simón Bolívar, the most fatherly image in the South American national imaginary (Long 1994). As carnival has become one of the central sites of representations of Brazilian nationalism, the figure of the transvestite has become prominent in the image of Brazilianness. The Neomexicanist School is an artistic movement in Mexico whose major proposal is to include queer subjects in the inventory of national subjects. These are some of the most visible interventions of the queer artistic production and they clearly deal with the national contention of the queer subject. The queer criticism of the nation has been one of the most important interventions intended to open the doors of citizenship to queer bodies.

This process of inclusion not only affects the queer population itself but also consists of a deep transformation in the framework of gender and sexuality that sustains patriarchy. This brings us to the political struggle for the legalization of practices and the assignation of rights traditionally reserved for heterosexual population. This deheterosexualizing of the law conveys a process of deheterosexualizing the state as well, and, in the long term, it sets out the path to removing the endemic relationship between patriarchy and the state. Nationalizing queer subjectivities, then, has an effect that goes beyond the minority rights field to a structural reconfiguration of patriarchy-ruled politics and culture. In E. K. Sedgwick's (1990) terms, the presumed sexual minority tends to be universalized. This does not mean that the increasing visibility of sexual diversity in Latin American media and the approval of important law reforms that recognize equal rights for nonheterosexual populations have reduced homophobic violence in the region. The efforts to achieve rights and inclusion have clashed with the naturalized oppression of patriarchy. In my analysis of this political unrest between citizenship aspirations and heterosexist reaction, the project of inclusion of dissident sexual and gender expressions is also conceived as an antihomophobic agenda that is concomitant with the general politics of human rights.

In spite of its Westernizing status, LGBT politics is experienced as a liberation saga. Nevertheless, recent scholarship and activism have turned to local systems of knowledge and practice, as they offer other categories that problematize the universal assumption of the modern Western sex–gender system. Queer Western politics tends to conceive bodies from a liberal and universalist perspective. In a different direction from this civilizatory narrative, scholarship on native sexualities opens up the discussion of non-Western sexualities and aims to decolonize questions of gender, sexuality, and uses of the body. At the same time, native queer politics challenges the notion of nation to prioritize the notion of community, and it also challenges the notion of universalizing the Western sex–gender system, instead prioritizing multicultural practices of sexuality. The utopia of universal liberation promises to lead to a global continuum of LGBT culture, which for various critics corresponds to the global expansion of the neoliberal economic system. On the other hand, the utopia of multiculturalism and decolonization looks for practices and conceptions of non-Western cultures as a way to escape the coloniality of gender and sex. Out of utopian constructions, an increasingly critical community has focused its interest on finding the place of sexuality in subaltern cultures in times of neoliberalism, as discussed in next section.

The machineries of consumption and disposability of neoliberalism complicate the processes of body liberation and queer expressions

Questions regarding the scope of queer theory in the neoliberal era are challenging, to say the least. If we maintain the liberationist or vindicationist view of the twentieth-century civil rights movements, queer theory and politics assign to the word *queer* a positive meaning of improvement of life conditions and social relations. This is the political sense of the LGBT movements. In the neoliberal era, the peripheral spaces—the ones we locate as the in-between places—have produced a form of exploitation that, because they deviate from the rules of patriarchal and heterosexual systems, can be defined as queer, although as a non-championable cause. Sex slavery, child pornography, pedophilia, sex tourism, and violent sexuality are forms of body exploitation and violations of human rights that signal one of the most disastrous effects of the market hegemony in present times. In her analysis of extreme capitalism, *Capitalismo gore*, the Mexican philosopher Sayak Valencia Triana (2010) reflects on a form of capitalism that bases its accumulation of wealth on the consumption and destruction of subaltern people's bodies.

In view of the rampant growth in Latin America of these forms of forced sexuality, in which the subject does not perform the sexual practices willingly, we need to deal with the ethics and politics of the troubling zones of the culture of the body. Latin American studies cannot ignore this emergent phenomenon, and indeed it has not ignored it in scholarship on gender and sexual violence produced in the past few decades across various disciplines. It is my intention to retrieve in this study various perspectives on the violent practices of sex and their connection to criminal neoliberalism or *capitalismo gore* (Valencia Triana 2010: 49–50). The archive concerned with these forms of coercive sexuality includes narratives related to sex abuses under the dictatorships in the region, especially in Guatemala and the Southern Cone; reports on femicides in Mexico, Central America, Brazil, and Argentina; works related to sex slavery trade in the Caribbean, Mexico, Central America, and the Southern Cone; analyses of the sex tourism economy in Mexico and the Caribbean; and reports on child pornography in Mexico (Altman 2001; Cacho 2006; Cruz-Malavé and Manalansan 2002; Domínguez Ruvalcaba 2007).

Addressing these areas of body exploitation has enabled a confluence of feminist, queer, postcolonial, and decolonial perspectives. The studies of the body, including the dead body, in the era of what Achille Mbembe (2003) calls "necropolitics," represents a great challenge to academic agendas related to the study of gender, race, and migration, to name three of the most important areas of debate at present. The confluence of views and epistemic positions around the enslaved and killed people of our times, and the very fact we are witnessing the construction of a society that perceives itself as victimized, urges a reorganization and redefinition of the role of sexuality, gender, and body studies in collective efforts to instate freedom from this violent system.

CHAPTER 1

Queer decolonization

The theoretical contributions to the studies of the colonial Latin American queer—or the queering of the colonial—in the conversations of Latin Americanist academia can be summarized as follows: a) queerness in Latin America is seen as a process of cultural translation whereby the multiplicity of pre-Columbian erotic practices is reduced to a normativized system of sexuality as a political strategy of control of bodies (or a biopolitics); b) colonizers deem nonreproductive sexualities sinful and condemnable/punishable, which in turn enables the emergence of hybrid, underground sexual practices that constitute an archive of the abject; c) indigenous third-sex theory reveals the conflict between a Western binary gender system and the three-sex system of some Amerindians, exposing homophobia as a colonial strategy; d) and a queer decolonizing proposal would aim not necessarily to reconstruct a native ancestral sex–gender system but rather to dismantle coloniality and disrupt its exclusionary and violent effects. In this chapter, my objective is to review some of the key ideas that have oriented discussions on the queer implications of coloniality.

Coloniality and queerness:
A discursive invasion

Since the 1990s, several academic discussions have developed around the postcolonial condition of Latin America, mainly animated by readings of subalternist South Asian scholars but, more importantly, by the questions that emerged after the end of the Cold War and the advent of neoliberalism. Marxism, psychoanalysis, and structuralism were well established as the prevalent theoretical frameworks in the humanities and social sciences for understanding Latin American realities during the Cold War period. However, new questions emerged after what Jorge Castañeda (1993) calls the disarmament of the utopia. Long-term agendas (such as psychoanalysis, Marxism, and structuralism) that had informed the capitalism–socialism contradiction now began to address questions of gender and sexuality, along with race, disability, and other minority issues in Latin America. By the end of 1980s, studies on gender, sexuality, racial issues, youth cultures, and migrations had taken hold in academic environments with increasing levels of transnational exchange, paving the way toward a transdisciplinary, transnational, and subalternist mode of knowledge production. The epistemic turn from class struggle and alienation to an axis based on the colonial brought about the inclusion of questions about the subject, the body, and multiculturalism in Latin Americanist research agendas. Contradictions and differences between exogenous cultures are deepened in times of neoliberal politics and global reconfigurations of markets and cultures.

Two events relating to bodies ignited the prominent academic incursion into the study of sexuality: the increasing number of serial killings of women in the continent made gender studies and feminist activism intensify their presence and influence in the public sphere, and the AIDS pandemic activated discussions on sexual identity and homophobic violence. These two immediate emergencies precipitated several forums that gathered academics from Latin American, European, and US universities, and those present began a transnational exchange addressing issues under postcolonial and subalternist theoretical reconfigurations. Unlike conventional disciplinary approaches, the emergent academic discourse was inclined to interrogate rather than to give answers, to deconstruct rather than to make assertions, and to cross disciplines rather than to narrow its work under a single disciplinary field.

It was then a palatable enterprise to review and ultimately to rewrite the history of the continent by returning to the literary, cultural, and historical canon. Critics searched in the canon for the keys to Latin America's colonial condition, the formation of the nation, the construction of repressive apparatuses, and the archeology of pleasures and perversions. The colonial condition, or coloniality, refers to the persistence of contradictions and forms of domination in multicultural, postcolonial societies, regardless of institutional and government changes (Quijano 2000). Sexual domination is one of the most significant forms of colonial interaction between colonizers and colonized. To name just one example, the trope of rape appears in various analyses as a foundational narrative of the mestizo culture.[1] What we might call a coloniality of sex, following Aníbal Quijano's (2000) notion of coloniality, refers to the punishment of difference as a way of correcting gender expressions and sexual practices. Sexuality, then, seems to be at the center of a multifaceted violence that includes physical pain, fear, exclusion, invisibility, moral condemnation, and even death. Colonial biopolitics has developed a complex bureaucracy, punishment techniques, and a discursive apparatus

---

[1] The most widely known work in this respect is Octavio Paz's *Labyrinth of Solitude* (published 1950). Rape is a leitmotif in nineteenth-century foundational novels such as *Iracema*, by Brazilian José de Alencar (published 1865), and *Cumandá: un drama entre salvajes*, by the Equadorian Juan León Mera (published 1879).

aimed at devaluing the colonized body. We cannot conceive of a Latin American sex–gender system without considering the traces of trauma left on colonized bodies; their painful expression would nurture a specific sensibility in the popular arts, as Mexican American scholar Laura Gutiérrez (2010) asserts in her work on the Mexican artist Astrid Hadad's performance (4).

The relation between the queer and the colonial can be seen as a question of transculturation of the body through the public policy of the colonial state. To subject sex to strict codes of mandatory heterosexuality is a colonizing action. Queerness is found in the interstices of cultural differences, the gaps left in translation. In the first place, queerness is not what describes the nonreproductive sexual practices admitted or tolerated in the native cultures of America; instead, I want to argue that queerness starts with the estrangement and condemnation of native sexual cultures, making criminal and sinful practices that used to be sinless. To expel, to condemn, to render invisible, and finally to proclaim their extermination ultimately engenders a zone of proscription, a zone defined by the unspeakable act of the body, which becomes abject. Queer people are noncitizens, they must cause revulsion, and their rejection is deemed pious, official, and mandatory.

If sexuality is not to be mentioned, it cannot be found in the archives, or only in the form of condemnation. Otherwise, there is not any category in the colonial archives that refers to the proscribed sexualities. The methodology of constructing knowledge of that which is unclassified consists of collecting the textual fragments spread all around the literature of and about Latin America, and interpreting the silences wherever sexual infractions are suggested. A careful rereading of the canonized works of literature and history and the review of legal codes, confessional manuals, and criminal archives are the routes scholars have taken to trace that zone of the colonial abject or what we call the colonial queer.

Queer colonial and translation

The queer colonial subject was formed as the result of a cultural process of translation in which native sexual conceptions were reduced to Christian rule. American historian Pete Sigal's (2007) essay "Queer Nahuatl: Sahagún's Faggots and Sodomites, Lesbians and Hermaphrodites" offers a keen analysis of the translation process deployed in the *Florentine Codex*. Bernardino de Sahagún's translation team—which included children of the Nahua nobility educated in the Franciscan school of Tlatelolco—drew and wrote this text in the late sixteenth century in New Spain (Mexico) (Sigal 2007: 10). The collaborative bilingual project includes illustrations, Latinized Nahuatl text, and a Spanish translation of that text. The codex itself shows the steps of the translation process, from pictograms to a Latin-alphabet Nahuatl transcription (a step that effectively reduces a multilayered graphic text to a word or phrase), and from the Latinized Nahuatl text to the Spanish version (a second step that simplifies the Amerindians' multiple sexual practices to the execratory term "nefarious sin," reinforcing the binary configuration of Europe's moral system).

Sigal's analysis focuses on how the criteria that organize the Nahuatl-into-Spanish translation are governed by the religious need to repress sexual practices. Sahagún and his team decided what to say and what to keep silenced according to religious and political interests. One result of this strategy is that we often find the retelling of Indian stories within a Judeo-Christian mythology. The colonial practice of translation reinvents the Indian world (even the word "Indian" is a colonial invention, a simplification of a multifarious and complex world) and controls the archive of the defeated civilization by pursuing specific political goals. For instance, several stories reported by the friars and conquerors from different regions of Latin America coincide to tell the disgraces of giant sodomites who were extinguished by plagues before the

Spaniards came (Bazán 2004: 64–66). The fact that the same biblical-resembling plot appears in the Spanish narratives of very different geographical regions shows how far colonial translation can go toward displacing local cultural memory, forging a convenient past for the colonizers. Translation is a twofold process—a disarticulation and a rearticulation of a cultural text. It is a writing, a political process whereby the system of meanings and values that would control colonial society is strategically resemanticized, enacting an erasure of a native sexual culture in order to force it into a restrictive mandatory heterosexuality.

By using the concept of "authorial filter," Sigal (2007) applies a methodology of reading the process of translation in order to uncover the process of colonization of sexuality (13). Sigal underscores two forms of sexually colonizing translation: the reduction of a variety of sexual practices to the words *sodomita* (sodomite) and *puto* (faggot) and the change in affective value the Spanish words hold when compared to the original Nahuatl. To illustrate the latter, the word *xochihua*, which in Nahuatl would mean literally "the flower bearer," in the *Florentine Codex* was translated as *puto* (faggot). Native categories are silenced and subsumed to the colonizer's categories. Colonizing translation is an act of epistemic violence that affects the very foundation of the meaning system. The violent effect of this translation consists of placing the body under a scrutinizing discipline imposed by the colonizer as a form of political control.

However, this violent subjugation to a discipline meets resistance in the cultural response to colonization. According to Sigal (2007), the fact that the concept of sin did not have any equivalence in the Nahua cultural system prevented the strategies for disciplining the body from neatly acculturating Amerindian sexuality; instead, a hybrid sexual system was created, one that still survives today in many indigenous and mestizo communities (13). Although Sigal does not offer further details about how this hybridity happens or where we can go to find instances of it, I would like to take his insight as a point of departure to argue that, by overcoming the constraints of the disciplinary/punitive framework with this hybridity, colonized sexuality is a place of identity formation. This identity emerges, then, in the interstices of the clash between a diversity of race, ethnicity, gender, and moral systems. Proscribed sexual practices become secret and residual. Their documentation in the criminal archives of the church and in civil government allows scholars to collect textual fragments about instances of sexual dissidence under colonial repression.

In his analysis of queer transculturation throughout different periods of colonial writing in the Andes, Michael Horswell (2005) asserts that the transcultured writers who produced the colonial indigenous accounts of pre-Columbian cultures occupy a queer space, as read in his comment on the seventeenth-century historian Santacruz Pachacuti:

> His singular narrative is barely intelligible to an uninitiated reader of Andean colonial writings by newly converted indigenous historians, whose language, style, and world view can be characterized as queer, that is, as eccentric to the Spanish metropolis' official histories and suspicious of even his indigenous contemporaries' versions of history. His text is queer in another sense of the word, that is, as it applies to what I consider to be the "subaltern knowledge" cryptically transmitted by the author in this text, knowledge that challenges his contemporaries' versions of Inca history, mythology, and, especially, Andean gender and sexual cultures. (140)

Horswell locates the queer colonial in the interstices of cultures and languages. Based on these assertions we can argue that the very process of cultural translation is in fact a queer process because of its refusal to adhere to the imperial dogma of sex and gender and because of its self-conscious suspicions regarding misrepresenting native gender culture. This in-between space recalls the queer bordering space of Gloria Anzaldúa (1999), in which identity consists of a continuous performance of translation itself. Horswell notes that the logic of these queer cultural liminal spaces is characterized by its eccentricity and its suspicion of misrepresentation. The narratives by Andean Christianized indigenous writers to which Horswell refers detail the role of androgynous and transgendered characters in pre-Columbian rituals. The depiction of third-sex subjects in these narratives demonstrates the centrality of androgynous and effeminate characters in Andean mythology. Catholic surveillance did not prevent these characters from being incorporated into the traditional Andean ceremonies and rituals that still take place today.

Paradoxically, it is in the sphere of the major control of consciences that sex talk happens. At the Catholic confessional, intimate sexual practices are continually interrogated, and thus a space for talking about sex, fantasies, desires, and fears is established. It is a space of interdiction derived from the moral struggle under the control machinery of colonial power; diverse bodily practices in a multicultural environment are put within a Western signifying regime by colonial authority. The obsessive interest of the church in knowing the intimate concerns of the population can be understood as a strategy of control of bodies (or biopower, in Foucauldian terms); as a way of gauging the effectiveness of acculturation or evangelization; or as an opportunity for sexual encounter between confessor and parishioners, extending colonial sexual violence to clerical spaces. The practices of surveillance of colonized bodies reveal that colonizing power is multifaceted: it controls souls, supervises the civilizing process, and sexually consumes colonized bodies.

The works of Michael Horswell (2005), Noemí Quezada (1989), and Pete Sigal (2007) read translation as a way of colonizing the very meaning of sexuality. In sum, colonization consists of disarticulating the epistemological, affective, and moral structure of preconquest so as to establish a new order of categories, a restrictive frame of coherence under which the fragments of a disarticulated culture persist and take place in the non-written discourses, or performances, of subalterns. Horswell's study of the *tinkuy*, or the third sex in Andean pre-Columbian culture, is based on the traces that the masculine-centered colonial order left visible. He chooses the ritual performances where the *tinkuy's* cross-dressed character is prominent. By addressing the performance, Horswell leaves the written archive in the background and concentrates on what Mexican scholar Diana Taylor (2003) calls the repertoire, that permanent set of symbols and narratives that is always updated according to the political and cultural tensions of the present (20). The third sex is nearly erased and transcultured, Horswell (2005) asserts (4). As in the colonized translation pinpointed by Sigal, Horswell is dealing with the residual. In the colonial structure the queer is repressed, denied, abject, and masked; in its proscribed space, however, the queer is represented by terms of condemnation and public scorn. This is the hybrid place of queer sexuality to which Sigal referred. It is a conflictive hybridity rather than the harmonious diversity of "mestizaje" as depicted in most official representations, as cultural critics such as Cornejo Polar and Yudice have pointed out (see Arroyo-Martínez 2003: 12–14). Cultural translation of any material related to sex and gender practice is scrutinized in this tense interaction between the colonizers and the colonized. Transculturation is visible in those bodily practices that the implacable repression of the colonial system renders possible. In this sense, colonial sexuality is the site of resistance for bodies subjugated by a moral discourse. This phenomenon is an object of attention in queer scholarship.

Noemí Quezada (1989) offers a suggestive method of analysis of proscribed cultural practices related to love and sexuality in Aztec culture. She investigates magic spells, rituals, and drug treatments so as to better understand the way pre-Columbian sexual conceptions are translated into the colonial order. Quezada reviews inquisitorial documents, confessional manuals, and chronicles in order to trace the manner in which pre-Columbian religions (whose ceremonies foregrounded sexuality prominently) and a series of social and economic activities related to sexuality were institutionalized and displaced by Christian sex-phobic doctrine. She then offers a view of the residual practices—considered magic and superstitions by colonizers—that remain (in partial form) of pre-Columbian ritual.

Quezada's review mentions homoerotic practices only twice, maybe due to the silence imposed on the nefarious sin, itself defined as the unspeakable. The first reference appears in her reading of the *Chant of Chalco Women*, an erotic and satiric Nahuatl poem intended to mock the Aztec emperor Axayacatl in celebration of the defeat of the Aztecs by the Chalco army. Throughout the poem, a group of women are trying to arouse Axayacatl, who remains indifferent to any stimulation. One of them reminds the king of his reputation of being "Eagle" and "Tiger" at the same time, an ambiguity that Quezada interprets as bisexuality. She also refers to the circulating gossip that Axayacatl sleeps with his enemies (Quezada 1989: 67). The homoerotic is used to demean the enemy, just as Federico Garza Carvajal (2003) has described in his analysis of the military discourse of the Spaniard cavalier in the colonial era (30). The homoeroticism disguised within these military metaphors may reveal some traces of the pre-Columbian same-sex practices associated with war. What we can infer from the text is a lack of condemnation of homoeroticism; it is rather a more gentle scolding of a mischievous behavior that causes a lack of sexual appetite: "Is it true you make mischief with your enemies?" (Quezada 1989: 67, my translation).

Another mention of homoeroticism in Quezada's work is in reference to a description of a magic spell found in a colonial text that represents the abduction by the god of the night (Tezcatlipoca) of the love goddess Xochiquetzal. In the last verse, Tezcatlipoca declares: "I myself am the young man, I'm the enemy. / But really I'm not the enemy: I'm femininity" (Quezada 1989: 73, my translation). Tezcatlipoca's gender ambiguity has drawn the attention of Pete Sigal in his analysis of the translation strategies in the *Florentine Codex*. For Sigal (2007), Fr. Bernardino de Sahagún (the leader of the translation team) misunderstands the complex nature of this god, effectively reducing Tezcatlipoca's identity to the Spanish derogatory word for homosexual, *puto* (26). By contrast, in Nahua culture's understanding of the god, Tezcatlipoca is a respected, powerful warrior and no derogatory words are used; having a sexual ambiguity does not diminish Tezcatlipoca's virility and power. The problem of the translation has to do with the affective aspect of meaning. *Culioni* (the Nahuatl word translated into Spanish as *puto*) only describes a man whose sexual practice consists of being penetrated by another man. The fact that the term *culioni* could be used to describe honored divinities such as Tezcatlipoca shows that sodomy was not a condemned behavior in the Nahua conception of sexuality. The Spanish version resorts to derogatory terms that only show that the act of translation functions as a strategy of rejection when it comes to issues of sexual diversity. Pete Sigal (2007) demonstrates how colonial translations hide the positive meanings of homoerotic practices in pre-Colombian Nahua culture by reducing them to condemnatory terms. In this case, evangelization triggers a process of devaluation and persecution of practices and bodily expressions that enjoyed approval and even privileges in the preconquest system.

Translation, functioning here as colonial political action over bodies, also operates on a poetic level by throwing into the zone of the unspeakable (*pecado nefando* or nefarious sin) a significant part of a culture. Expelling the queer identities *xochihua* and *tinkuy* from their place in Nahua and Quechua cultures, respectively, dehumanizes them. The colonizing process of making meaning does not stay on a purely rhetorical level; it is, as mentioned, a biopolitical strategy that involves a variety of disciplinary actions, such as spectacles of public scorn meant to serve as a lesson for virtual offenders or secret punishments for erotic practices intended to prevent the emergence of possible imitators. The flower bearers and the transvestite wise man were treated as practitioners of an unnatural and then unspeakable sin; they were expelled from what was deemed normal and were even removed from all forms of representation. Nefarious, unspeakable, counter-nature, and so forth were the concepts used to describe these figures; these negative concepts referred explicitly to a prohibition against being represented and to the condition of being outside the "normal," which in the monolithic culture of imperial Spain was a sufficient reason for exemplary public death: scorn in this context is the pious expression expected from the good Catholic citizen.

Reading the visceral

The vast silence about nonheterosexual sexuality defines this translation of sexual cultures. The history of queer bodies in Latin America is the history of the facts excluded from records, the history of that which is deemed nonhistorical. In that sense, writing a history of a colonization of bodies results in a history counter to mainstream colonial studies. In his essay "Visceral Archives of the Body," Zeb Tortorici (2014) reflects on the nature of the archive of proscribed sexualities in colonial Mexico. Tortorici looks at the criminal cases in which sexual transgressors confessed their sexual practices to authorities and were sometimes punished with a death sentence. The texts are nasty dialogues in which the confession produces repulsion; the story itself functions as an instrument for punishment. Queerness is then found in the visceral side of the judicial archives; the excrescence that emerges from those colonial documents was discarded from mainstream historical research and left untouched until a queer interest brought them into our academic discussion. The construction of a visceral archive, as Tortorici proposes, performs a completely different politics from the one it did when the confessions were actually written down. Queer criticism deals with marginalized bodily practices of the past and, by doing so, connects affectively with them. In that way, queer criticism produces a knowledge of the hidden side of the history of the body. Scholarship on the queer colonial aims to establish an archeology of queerness in Latin America; the colonial archives are an unavoidable source for understanding the factors that articulate the modern Latin American sex–gender system. By stating that queerness is an expression of coloniality, queer historians aim to trace the line of the decolonizing impulse since the time of its foundational repression.

The visceral nature of queer colonial archives, according to Tortorici (2014), enables an affective reading of sexual events through the repulsive reactions manifested by the scribes, the interrogators, the archivists, and even the historians (407). The abject reappears each time the document is read, making the repulsive reaction a constitutive part of queer textual production. The archive queers itself by recording and keeping those uncomfortable documents: "[t]he cases of necrophilia, fellatio, and sex with the Devil, holy images, and the Eucharist all present the colonial archive as a space that, in some regards, queers its own convention" (Tortorici 2014: 431). Criminal narratives describing judicial procedures against sexual differences are invaluable sources for historicizing the formation of queer spaces of meaning in Latin America. Colonial queerness is produced in the context of institutional actions against sexual difference. For bodily practices to be deemed queer, they have to be read as a defiance of the norm; their actions and desires are threats to the institutions that implement a biopolitical, administrative form of control over bodies. It can be argued, however, that the diversity of bodily practices exists independently from the norms that sanction them. Diego Falconí Trávez (2016), commenting on colonized populations whose culture included the figure of La Tunda—a queer mythological Amazonian character whom it is believed abducts people to sexually abuse them—resorts to mythological narratives to open up a space outside colonial repression (312).

The repressive colonial administrative machine has the effect of suppressing sexual identities and practices sanctioned by the preconquest order. At the same time (and perhaps counterintuitively), the ruling ideology itself generates queer fantasies, as in the visceral archive of Tortorici (2014). A similar dialectical relationship occurs in the sacred realm as well; sacrilegious fantasies involve the conversion of a religious object into an object of sexual desire. Both the suppressed sexual practice and the sacrilegious act perform queerness in the underworld of the colonial system. They are produced as illegal, forbidden, and dejected; the lives of their enactors are constrained to secret, invisible, and unstable spaces. (At least this is the location they occupy as represented within the criminal archives of queer, bodily practice.) In any case, opening the visceral archive of colonial records is itself a gesture of retrieving the proscribed, of finding in the margins of colonial history the very archeology of Latin American queerness. It is assumed in this archaeology that non-Western, nonpatriarchal, ancestral people enjoyed sexuality without guilt.

Third-sex theory, which informs Sigal's (2007) and Horswell's (2005) work, accentuates the contrast between the West's binary gender order and the multiplicity of the pre-Columbian one. The third-sex framework makes clear that colonization's cultural clash is centrally located in the contradictions and conflicts that occurred in the sexual and gendered fields. Decolonization, then, would have to deal with redefining and restructuring the discourses, rules, and practices of the body in order to effectively counter the colonial havoc wrought within Latin American society.

The third-sex trope is the main theoretical basis of Marinela Miano Borruso's (2003) ethnography of the *muxe'*, a queer gender assignation of Oaxaca, Mexico. Miano Borruso shows how the *muxe'* system opens up a gap within the dominant Catholic ideology that treats nonheterosexual sexualities as anathema, unpronounceable sinful acts. The unrepentant acceptance of *muxe'* is a feature of a pre-Colombian third-sex system that persists in the isthmus region as if it were untouched by the imposition of colonial binaries. Nevertheless, Miano Borruso asserts that Zapotec culture is not a monolithic, closed nation, anchored to its ancestral customs. It has taken from others a diversity of cultural elements and has appropriated them without losing its autonomy. Zapotecs want to be modern as long as they remain Zapotec (Miano Borruso 2003: 36–37). This ethnography places the third-sex model in another frame of reference beyond the pre-Columbian source. Miano Borruso underlines the flexibility of Zapotec gender conceptions in contrast to traditional homophobic Mexican culture; at the same time, she shows the influence of Western gay politics in the Zapotec community. In her description of the queer geography of the town of Juchitán, she observes that gays tend to be less visible in the most wealthy sector and that the trans population (characterized as *muxe'*) is concentrated in the working-class area. Miano Borruso suggests a subtle colonialism of the Zapotec society along the lines of the traditional mestizo gender standards (i.e., the dominant culture of the country). In this analysis, *muxe'* culture is identified as a local ethnicity, affiliated with an ancestral Zapotec gender system. While the mestizo is related to modernization (marked as the professional, middle-class, gay-identified subject), the *muxe'* is an identity rooted in Zapotec culture, and its citizenship is legitimated in the discourse of indigeneity (Miano Borruso 2003: 159–160). Although their alternative gender expression is admitted, they are still far from proposing a clear politics against the patriarchal system of inequality. According to Miano Borruso, the *muxe'* express a frustrated desire to be treated as traditional women, often staying at home and depending on a husband who supports them (162). Does this mean that *muxe'* culture is part of a Zapotec patriarchal system and that it can in no way be considered part of the liberating agendas of feminist and LGBT movements? At most, we can observe in Miano Borruso's ethnography that Zapotec patriarchy is a much more benevolent one than mestizo's in terms of the level of acceptance of sexual diversity. Although part of the fantasy of the *muxe'* involves dressing like TV divas and wishing to marry as a traditional woman would, their place in society is one of respect and recognition of the Zapotec cultural heritage they represent. Often, Miano Borruso underlines the vaunted social position of the *muxe'* to insist on the contrast between the mestizo and the Zapotec. As in Horswell's (2005) study of the *tinkuy*, in Miano Borruso's study the very event of the performance itself constitutes the representational moment in which we can locate the elements of a queer indigenous subject and appreciate that subject's central place in social and religious rituals as well as in daily life. Through this strategy of contrasting the indigenous as the culture that assigns a place for a queer subject and the mestizo as a largely colonizing and repressive culture, Miano Borruso proposes a decolonizing way of signifying queerness. By having a place in the community and enjoying the prerogatives of indigenous identities, queer subjects are able to take on positions of leadership and power in their very difference. According to Miano Borruso, the *muxe'* are the main custodians of tradition within their community, leading the traditional saint-related *velas* (community fests) as well as the *velas* for the *muxe'* themselves, which were started in the 1970s. The *muxe'*, then, took over the leadership in order to enact a politics of ethnicity as a form of decolonization and of queering local politics at the same time. Where a colonizing sexuality is seen as the imposition of a binary system, the central role of the *muxe'* in keeping ethnic cultural expressions alive can be read as a decolonizing strategy. Miano Borruso's ethnography, then, can be taken as the articulation of a fully formed cultural system because the *muxe'* exist as a legitimate identity.

Miano Borruso (2003) reads Zapotec sexuality against the backdrop of mestizo culture. To explain some events of aggression against *muxe'*, Miano Borruso assigns blame to a westernized mestizo culture in which there exists no conceivable alternative to the heteronormative binary. Heterosexuality is the only admitted sexuality in the hegemonic mestizo gender system, even though homoerotic practice is overwhelmingly present. Despite the mestizo-dominated landscape, the phenomenon of the *muxe'* endures, located in the most pure extreme of the Zapotec cultural spectrum, where it is part of a traditional conception of gender (Miano Borruso 2003: 160). Miano Borruso is indeed referring to the gendered culture of the mestizo when she observes that the feminine model the *muxe'* try to emulate is not the strong, self-sufficient Zapotec woman but the docile, subjugated mestizo one (162).

It can be argued, however, that the *muxe'* diva fantasy reinstalls *muxe'* identity within the scope of coloniality. Miano Borruso records the intense cultural exchange between the mestizo, the national, and the international diva iconographies, aesthetic trends, and so on but at all times she emphasizes the place of the *muxe'* within a unique gender structure in which—as soon as the first signs of effeminacy are visible in their childhood—*muxe'* are trained to be *muxe'* by their mothers as a third-sex construction. The *muxe'* are highly appreciated in Zapotec society, especially by mothers, for having the mind of a man and the sensibility and industry of a woman. They are hard workers; they take care of children and elders and they contribute to the household better than heterosexual children (Miano Borruso 2003: 162–163).

But the education of a *muxe'* does not end in the home, as they also need to be a *muxe'* in the social sphere, where the interaction of a queer sexuality with a mestizo, homophobic culture raises many risks. In her analysis of the most important *muxe'* celebration, Vela de las auténticas intrépidas buscadoras de peligro (Vigil of the Authentic and Intrepid Danger-Seekers), Miano Borruso (2003) discovers a process of cultural translation that is visible in *muxe'* performance: a complex representation involving wardrobe, parody, and rituality allows the *muxe'* to arrive at a specific queer place that presents itself as an *endemic*, local gender expression. But a *muxe'* does not perform inside the specifically Zapotec scenario; she situates herself in the intersection of the Zapotec nonbinary gender system and the mestizo double-standard heteronormative constraints. Even though the ethnic legitimizing of the *muxe'* places queerness at the center of the symbolic performance of Zapotec identity, this centrality does not protect them against homophobic attacks, mostly from mestizos. They then need to learn how to defend themselves, physically, verbally, and through organized political action. The *muxe'* are reputed to combine the best of the woman and the best of the man. While mothers educate *muxe'* in the domestic and economic activities assigned to *muxe'* such as embroidery, cooking, selling goods in the market, and caregiving for children, elders, and the sick, it is the responsibility of the community of *muxe'* to train each other in individual and group self-defense. On the one hand, the education of the mothers is intended to preserve Zapotec tradition in the face of colonizing cultural pressure; on the other, they are educated by their peers in the political struggle, in the social and sexual realm, and against the structural violence of dominant patriarchy. *Muxe'* are educated to perform a double decolonizing fight: first, a fight for endurance through the preservation of the cultural elements that construct ethnicity and, second, a struggle of conflictive coexistence with homophobic culture. The latter has led to a continuous and systematic troubled state of culture in which, despite having existed in tandem for centuries, the irreconcilability of the mestizo binary gender system and the Zapotec third-sex conception hinders the possibility of a full cultural translation. The climate of tolerance this coexistence has precipitated does not prevent the *muxe'* from being at risk when the homophobic rules of dominant society are applied on them violently, as they have been since the time of the conquest.

Colonial heterogeneity can be depicted as a cultural and political battleground, a permanent state of tension in the multicultural experience in which coexistence is defined by conflict. Peruvian cultural and literary critic Antonio Cornejo Polar (2003) observes that narratives addressing indigenous cultures deal with the contradictions between nations (207). The *muxe'* group Intrepid Risk-Seekers in the Tehuantepec region is a collective movement that challenges hegemonic Mexican homophobia, not only by cross-dressing but also by appropriating political spaces in the community. This reveals one of the main roles of the *muxe'* in Zapotec culture: they do not seek acceptance from their community, which is taken for granted since they are already legitimized in their gender system; rather, they work to take over the leadership of the community, especially in those aspects of social life relating to the practices of Zapotec identity.

The complex cultural location of the *muxe'* illustrates the borders of sexual coloniality: by confronting homophobic mestizo attacks, the *muxe'* organize a type of decolonial action. The tension depicted in Miano Borruso's (2003) ethnography offers an instance of the epistemic colonial violence applied to cultural practices. According to Garza Carvajal (2003), cultural difference concerning sexuality provided an excuse for the colonial project, as it was another "just cause" for cultural domination (24). For him, the construction of imperial manliness was a strategy for the conquest of non-European cultures; even more, he deems the "prosecution of sodomites" to be "one [of the] constitutive principles of imperialism" (33). In his reading of catechist manuals used to evangelize the population subjugated following the Andean conquest, Horswell (2005) asserts that sodomy is one of the most obsessed-over topics in doctrinal literature and also one of the most punished and rejected behaviors. He notes that the biblical story of Sodom and Gomorrah is constantly compared to the destruction of Andean civilizations, as both narratives invoke cataclysm as a sign of God's anger toward the nefarious, unpronounceable, and abominable sin (Horswell 2005: 210–211). The reference to the nefarious sin in the characterization of the Amerindians in colonial narratives is notoriously abundant. A diverse sexual practice became, then, a triggering cause of invasion and destruction.

In his *Historia de la homosexualidad en la Argentina*, Osvaldo Bazán (2004) shows that the accusation of sodomy and the use of cruelty to punish are forms of pedagogy against what are understood as counter-nature sexual practices—practically, any nonreproductive sexuality is severely punished. For Bazán, these condemned sexual practices were admissible in many pre-Columbian cultures and even sanctioned as another gender identity, which coincides with Horswell's (2005) and Miano Borruso's (2003) findings. The process of conquest and colonization involved disciplining sexuality as a method of domination. In one of the earliest expeditions through the Panama Isthmus, commanded by Vasco Núñez de Balboa, Spaniards made their war-dogs devour a group of effeminate men from the native elite. Bazán's account of this and myriad other events related to the violence against "sodomites" in the conquest and colonization highlights the political use of sexuality and the body as one of the principal tactics of colonial expansion. The biopolitics of imperial Spain consisted of placing the body at the center of the colonial imaginary. Like Garza Carvajal (2003) and Horswell (2005), Bazán (2004) underlines the importance of the concept of sodomy, an all-purpose word that seems to include a diversity of nonapproved sexual practices in the Catholic doctrine that the Spaniards used to evangelize the natives. Colonizers claimed for themselves the mission of converting the infidels, hetero-normativizing their intimate life (i.e., imposing a norm over the body for political, colonial purposes) as a mechanism of domination through the control of practices related to biological functions of bodies, such as sexuality. Colonialism's clash of cultures necessitated the creation of a sexual code that reduced sexuality to one function (the reproductive one) and the establishment of a political system whose major concern was the somatization of the empire: as long as Spanish rule prohibited, blamed, and cruelly and spectacularly punished the transgressors, the dominion over the colonized was secured. Although the technology of war played a decisive role in the enterprise of conquest, the process of colonization would not have been successful without the biopolitics centralized on the control of sexuality. Scholars addressing queer issues of the colonial condition interpret queerness as the result of a system of disciplining the body in order to dominate it.

Centrality of the liminal

A multicultural environment defined by the accumulation of abuses is necessarily a field of cultural struggle. It is a commonplace to refer to this cultural plurality as a space of negotiation, a harmonious syncretism in which the very phenomenon of mixing races— mestizaje—will solve the conflicts between races. Essentially this optimism is embodied in the creole construction of the national imaginary of most Latin American countries. Canonical authors such as José Vasconcelos (1929) in Mexico with his concept of "cosmic race" and Sérgio Buarque de Holanda (1936) in Brazil with his concept of "the cordial man" (*o homem cordial*) believe that mestizaje has overcome the biases of the defenders of racial purity. However, this idealization of the mixed race prevents us from seeing that syncretism and hybridity are nothing but a continued series of politically driven translations, tactical misunderstandings, and conscious efforts to mislead. In a semantic space defined by many layers of cultural translation, meaning is necessarily quite unstable. The most prominent effect of this instability is a calling into question of colonial rule broadly speaking; also, we see a field of meaning characterized by a complex syncretism opening up, one in which native cultural strata find their way into the cultural negotiation, as many ethnographers of Latin American indigenous communities have discussed. Transculturation is one of the most accepted critical concepts used to define this liminal space (Alvarez 2014; Ortiz 1973).

For Horswell (2005), the process of transculturation in the sexual realm occurs in the intimate interrogation of the confessional. He observes three facets of this process: "how the confessional separated the penitent from his or her community; how confession separated him from his ritual practice; and how new notions of acceptable sexual behavior were introduced" (Horswell 2005: 212). The space of interdiction par excellence inserts colonial power into the native subjectivity by disarticulating community and rituality and by surveilling sexual behavior. Politics of disempowering communal cohesion, replacing religious and moral systems, and punishing the body coincide in the transculturation project. Religious culture and the establishment of new punishable behavioral codes of conduct work together in the assembly of a colonial machinery.

The accounts of sexual repression in colonial history and their resonances in present-day ethnographies of sexuality describe a colonizing force that broke apart any institutional systems that did not repress several specific sexual practices (arguably this would characterize the majority of pre-Columbian nations). However, to invoke an idealized ancestry in which sexuality was not repressed and patriarchy did not exist only amounts to a political strategy comparable to the idealization of the mestizaje as embodying harmonizing race interrelations, mentioned above. In his discussion of the invisibility of HIV/AIDS in indigenous communities, Mexican anthropologist Guillermo Núñez Noriega (2011) observes it is a generalized perception that, because Amerindians are thought to be close to nature, homosexuality has not spread among them. While the conquerors used any suspected sodomy as an excuse for invading and dispossessing the natives, the indigenous advocates Núñez Noriega interviewed were reluctant to talk about sexual diversity in their communities for fear that the stigmatization used against them could become even worse (Núñez Noriega 2011: 16–17). Nature and ancestry are then tropes of a metaphysics for (not) discussing indigenous sexuality, but the two tropes are contradictory: while the former is used to demonstrate Amerindians are close to nature and thus cannot be homosexuals, the latter tries to erase possible discourses that would admit the existence of a pre-Columbian heterosexual patriarchy.

Lorena Cabnal, a Mayan communitarian feminist, admits there is a millenarian, ancestral, Mayan patriarchy that is repurposed when in contact with Western patriarchy; she and other communitarian feminists such as the Bolivian Julieta Paredes call this phenomenon the *entronque patriarcal* (patriarchal junction) (see Gargallo 2014: 18–19). Their conception of a double patriarchy allows us to suggest that a Latin American gender system cannot be understood without drawing a map of a chain of oppressive, conflictive, and seductive relations in which race, class, ethnicity, and sexuality, among other marks of identity, intersect. In this complex intersectionality plotted in the colonial system, the queer body, the most rejected subject since the conquest saga, is for that very reason a canvas upon which colonial hate was obsessively inscribed. While the systematic oppression of heretics, idolaters, and Jews ceased after the Holy Office and colonial administration were replaced by liberal institutions, the repudiation of the sexual and gender dissidents continues to the present, constituting the most dominant feature of the current coloniality of sex. In effect, the coloniality of sex, whose most prominent expression is the punishment of difference, is the most supported form of exclusion across the entire social spectrum.

Rita Segato (2011) offers a suggestive interpretation of transformations within the gender system of Latin America following Western colonization, laying out two central processes. Firstly, Segato notes that an existing Amerindian patriarchy was enhanced by the colonial introduction of a Western patriarchy that increased intolerance of sexual difference and female agency. Segato's second assertion is the central axis, as described in this chapter, of colonial queer studies: in several Amerindian nations, a third sex was institutionalized. Segato is responding to Eurocentric feminism that conceives of patriarchy as universal, as well as positions such as those of María Lugones (2007) and Oyeronke Oyewumi (1997), who assert that a patriarchal gender order was nonexistent in the precolonial period (Segato 2011: 31–32). According to Segato, the arrival of Western patriarchy meant a painful reconstitution of gender relations and norms of sexual practices. Needless to say, examples of this new imposed sexual order abound: the objectification of women's bodies and the criminalization of sexual diversity are expressions of the pornographic character of the colonizer's gaze.

Federico Garza Carvajal (2003) focuses on the oppression of queer bodies within the colonial system, recovering the discourse of pain that has nurtured the criticism of torture of native bodies from Bartolomé de Las Casas to the literature of *testimonio* in post-Cold War Latin America.[2] A look through the main scholarship on Latin America reveals how centrally a discourse of pain dominates the analysis of culture and politics. Trauma, scars, resentment, and

---

[2] *Testimonio* is a literary form based on oral narrations of people who lived or witnessed events and conditions that either are erased or misrepresented in conventional history and literature.

torture become the articulatory metaphors used to understand political phenomena such as military dictatorships, misogynist and homophobic violence, racial exclusion, and migratory conflicts. Trauma and its most closely affiliated genre, the *testimonio*, have nurtured a politics of human rights and subaltern empowerment, which analyses have found evident in Southern Cone dictatorships, in the abuses of guerrilla groups, in paramilitary and organized crime in Colombia, in critical treatments of femicides in the Mexican–US border zone, and in the gross human slaughter during the Guatemalan, Nicaraguan, and Salvadoran civil wars. Similarly, Gloria Anzaldúa (1999) uses the metaphor of the open scar to refer to the painful uprooting of migrant populations and the unrest of living "in between." The trope of the body in pain (Scarry 1985) also informs the scholarship on what we can call the colonial condition of the queer body.

In his substantial review of the archive of sodomy-related judicial processes in early modern Spain and New Spain, Garza Carvajal (2003) compiles a series of archival documents describing interrogations, events of public scorn, and the cruelties of torture and execution. The fierceness of punitive actions speaks to how capitally important the regulation of dissident sexualities was to the process of colonization. The so-called sins against nature (sodomy, anthropophagy, incest, and human sacrifice) served as a type of "just cause" rationale for the conquest. The extreme and spectacular nature of the torture against the sodomite itself proves that the colonizers viewed these so-called sinful actions as detestable. For Garza Carvajal (2003), the spectacle of punishment functioned as a mechanism to make the colonized population believe in the supremacy and desirability of *vir*, the idealized heterosexual Hispanic–Catholic warrior man (104). To reiterate, this characterization of colonial order does not negate the fact that pre-Hispanic indigenous culture might have developed a form of patriarchy that ruled its gender and power relations; Garza

Carvajal only suggests that Hispanic patriarchy imposed a series of hierarchies: men over women, heterosexual over homosexual, and Spaniard and European men over Amerindians, blacks, and mestizos. Thus, colonization can be defined as a reconfiguration of body politics in such a way that sexuality, race, ethnicity, and religion intersect in the practices of exclusion, oppression, and dispossession of the human bodies of the colonies.

Decolonial trends in Latin Americanist discourses emphasize coloniality as the articulatory principle of oppression, replacing the centrality of capitalism that dominated the Marxist analyses of the Cold War academy. In his introduction to the book *Violencias (re)encubiertas en Bolivia* by Silvia Rivera Cusicanqui (2010), Sinclair Thomson considers this epistemological turn as a new form of interpreting Latin American history in terms of coexistent temporalities, questions of differing citizenship, and an internal colonialism present in the quotidian micropolitics of colonial inequalities and exclusions (14). In her interpretation of the effects of colonial rules in the Bolivian gender system, Rivera Cusicanqui underlines that the colonial process generated a crisis in Andean societies concerning normativity (191). Mestizaje, the race mixing that characterizes colonial demography, is not a solution to racial segregation; it only represents a space of condemnation and self-denying subjectivity. For Rivera Cusicanqui, the fact that most mestizos were born illegitimately, as the result of sexual abuses by Spaniards on indigenous women, allowed mothers the opportunity to establish rules within their own fatherless households. This new normativity within the illegitimate families of colonial domination constitutes a "third republic," a bridge between the colonizers and the indigenous cultures, as it is the indigenous mother who educates the mestizo, but neither inside the orthodoxy of indigenous tradition nor in the environment of the ruling Spaniards (Rivera Cusicanqui 2010: 194). Still, within the liminal space of the mestizo, Rivera Cusicanqui observes a polarized society, rather than an organized "republic," in which some mestizos live under different universes of reference given their multiple cultural heritages (195–196). This space should not be characterized as a conciliatory solution to colonial segregation, as official discourses have asserted, but as a space populated by many contradictions and conflicts described using such terms as "conflictive heterogeneity" (Cornejo Polar 2003), "internal colonialism" (González Casanova 1969), "masks" (Paz 2004), "mimicry" (Bhabha 1994), and "cultural transvestism" (Arroyo-Martínez 2003). The increasing population of mestizos in most Latin American societies suggests that this mix of cultural ambivalence and instability determines norms of conduct and meaning systems to be subsidiary to official rules and formal discourses. The coloniality of sex has its foundation in the contradiction between the repressive rule of the colonizer and the emerging "third republic," which is a resistant reaction to the act of sexual violence that founded the mestizo society. I want to argue that this third republic can also be described as a process of queering the colonial rules over bodies (a decolonial transgression of the colonial system of oppression) and, at the same time, a process of altering the indigenous rules themselves: Miano Borruso's (2003) ethnography on the *muxe'* is quite illustrative of this double queering that the third republic model implies.

Cultural analysis shows how the colonized queer complicates our understanding of subaltern colonized culture. Gloria Anzaldúa (1999) proposes that queer culture might be best served by escaping the dominion of Mexican American patriarchy entirely. The condition of being marginal to an already marginal community places the queer in a very troubled zone of identity. Nevertheless, if a lack of unity characterizes subaltern communities, as Gramsci (1971: 52) suggests, being queer is not exceptional but a norm in the multicultural and conflictive Latin American society. The heteronormative ruling elite in migrant communities has been indoctrinated in a culture of Catholic colonial homophobia, has created the instruments of punishment and condemnation of the queer body, and has imposed them over subaltern bodies. Queer politics would then be a decolonizing energy that emerges as a force of resistance to the colonial normative regime that established punitive politics regarding sexual dissidence; queer politics forms as a direct consequence of the body being in pain. This punitive culture remains in place in present-day Latin America even though antidiscriminatory laws have been approved in the majority of the countries in the region. This permanent social structure, which insistently excludes sexual diversity, is what is being referring to with the term "coloniality of sex."

Miano Borruso's (2003) ethnography of the *muxe'* shows the tensions between their family-supported alternative sexuality and the Westernized Christian and macho homophobia of their mestizo neighbors: it is a moral entanglement that defines the subjectivities of the *muxe'*. Rivera Cusicanqui (2010) and Miano Borruso (2003) coincide in presenting the mother as a source of support for queer sexualities, establishing a counterhegemonic family in which dominant normativity is necessarily adapted to the illegitimate condition, enabling alternative forms of gender and sexualities. For both authors, fathers are absent or at least they are not determiners in the gender education of their offspring. For Rivera Cusicanqui, the formation of the illegitimate mestizo provides a basis for a rebellious subjectivity that determines a rancorous sensibility and ultimately a revolutionary agency; for Miano Borruso, the *muxe'* are Zapotec cultural advocates and themselves champions of counterhomophobic politics.

The liminal fields of Rivera Cusicanqui's (2010) third republic and of Anzaldúa's (1999) borderlands nurture a transcultured conception of gender, giving colonization and decolonization a bodily concreteness. To summarize, the postcolonial body can be conceived of as a subject that is not quite dominated nor quite liberated. In this in-between status, the efforts to control the subaltern body have entailed the formation of a complex institutional apparatus, or what Foucault (1980) calls a "dispositif," which includes a number of strategies of discipline, censorship, co-option, indoctrination, criminalization, enslaving, and pathologization. All of these practices, norms, and discourses are components of what Latin Americanist academia has defined as coloniality.

Colonial dispositif informs and causes a discourse of resistance as a dialectical continuum of subjection and transgression in which sexuality—its normativity and its perversion—is the carnal signifier, the somatic sign expressed in desire and punishment. These disciplinary colonial institutions provide the conditions that precipitate the formation of a margin of dissidence, an underground practice of condemned sexual and gender expressions. Two paradigmatic characters frame Garza Carvajal's (2003) historical analysis of sodomy in early modern Hispanic society: Catalina de Erauso, who became a second lieutenant of the Spanish Royal Army with the masculine name of Alonso or Antonio Díaz, and Juan de la Vega, a mulatto effeminate man from Mexico City who preferred being named "Cotita." Both individuals, Garza Carvajal (2003) concludes, "might have contested gender roles in Spain–New Spain, but they nonetheless affirm the state's discourses about manliness" (188). While Erauso embraced all the *vir* values that embodied the state's and the church's norms of maleness, de la Vega/"Cotita" and others enacted the habits and style of the most celebrated women of colonial high class. These subaltern subjects, who transgress and imitate at the same time the very image of their oppressors, reveal many internal contradictions in the colonial regime; it becomes necessary to think about replacing the established set of sex/gender roles with a very fluid space in which bodily affairs depend deeply on the political unrest that characterizes multicultural, colonized, or postcolonized societies.

Gender, sex, and race intersect in the formation of subaltern identities, although their expression often mimics hegemonic gender ideals (the Spaniard warrior in the case of Catalina de Erauso, the high-class woman in the case of Juan de la Vega, and TV divas in the case of the *muxe*). The bastard mestizo (not to mention the Mexican Malinche) is a problematic and contradictory subject that may connote treason or rebelliousness, mendacity or heroism. Defined by its instability, this figure has become a frequent trope of the Latin American essayist tradition. For example, in *El Perfil del hombre y la cultura en México*, Samuel Ramos (1982) discusses the *peladito*, a subaltern character who is a completely dispossessed individual who speaks a meaningless language and is only able to survive through his ability to deceive and trick (52–61). In Octavio Paz's (2004) well-known depiction of the rancorous mestizo, the fact that he is a mixture of a lonely orphan and a resented bastard provides sufficient explanation for his hermetic and eventually violent psyche (89–90). A similar morally troubled identity is depicted in the work of Chilean author Sonia Montecino (1996), who notes that Chilean families established since the colonial era are often polygamist and mother-centered (47). These works coincide with Rivera Cusicanqui's (2010) ideas on gender formation in Bolivian society, where subaltern morality emerges in the mother-centered family and is marked by illegitimacy.

I adopt the conflictive, uncomfortable notion of the mestizo instead of the harmonious one the political elites and official intellectuals have propagated. The liminal character of mestiza consciousness in Gloria Anzaldúa's seminal *Borderland/La frontera* (1999) reflects on how the mestiza is problematically related to the nation, the hegemonic gender system, and even language itself as she is always located between meaning systems, at the uncomfortable moment of the translation. In *Borderland/La Frontera*, Anzaldúa finds that exacerbating differences is a path to neutralizing the segregating network of identities. Whereas segregation consists of excluding and contrasting identities, the radical difference we can find in Anzaldúa is a sum of many differences. The crossroads of queerness takes gender and racial differences into a broader inclusiveness: "As lesbian I have no race, my own people disclaim me; but I am all races because there is the queer of me in all races" (Anzaldúa 1999: 102). Racial difference for Anzaldúa is overcome by the queerness present in all races; queerness shows an intersubjective inside where differences are redefined as a desirable feature rather than a mark of segregation. Queerness calls hegemonic notions of race and gender into question by transforming the significance of difference. In her preface to *This Bridge We Call Home* (2015), Anzaldúa proposes building bridges that cross racial and gender classifications (2–3). In *Borderland/La Frontera*, she introduces a political statement that breaks down the barriers of identity: "[t]he new *mestiza* copes by developing a tolerance for contradictions, a tolerance for ambiguity" (1999: 101). Analouise Keating (1998) observes that Anzaldúa "transforms essentialized conceptions of identity into transcultural, transgendered models of subjectivity. By positing the non-duality of self and other, they construct multilayered discourses recognizing both the diversities *and* commonalities between and among apparently dissimilar people" (31). In other words, developing this tolerance for contradictions and ambiguity enables Anzaldúa not only to redefine oppositional differences but also to state that contradictions and ambiguities can become the liberating conditions of humanism and sources of creativity.

The notion of queer as an ethnic and gender multiplicity implies a politics of difference that subverts the segregating order. Antihomophobic interventions, as Eve K. Sedgwick (1990: 9–10) proposes, need to target a binary system of exclusion (heterosexual vs. homosexual, masculine vs. feminine, white vs. nonwhite or people of color), demonstrating that such a binary distribution is asymmetrical. In fact, most of our social categorizations are based on uneven relationships. Starting from Anzaldúa's propositions, it is possible to suggest that queer decolonization focuses on that system of differences, making visible the obsolescence of a binary asymmetrical order and emphasizing the importance of building bridges in order to neutralize exclusionary practices. According to this perspective, there is an enveloping community that overcomes interethnic and international segregation. The queer perspective represents a way to blur oppositional categorization, precisely confronting "the traits and habits distorting how you see reality and inhibiting the full use of your facultades" (Anzaldúa 2002b: 541).

Coming out of US queer-of-color academia, the decolonizing queer perspective's utopian horizon envisioned an inclusive notion of identity and citizenship, replacing an oppositional logic to allow for what Anzaldúa (2002b) calls a "new tribalism," in which oppressed subjects, the others of a repressive coloniality, build bridges between one another (3). The intersection of sex and ethnicity and the construction of bridges between the oppressed and the excluded constitute an epistemic and political program that more or less defines today's transnational intellectual agenda, which can be summarized as follows:

a) Deconstructing heterosexual hegemony involves the critique of a system of exclusion and prejudices that constitutes the modern state. When oppositional categorizations do not make sense any more, heterosexuality will not be the a priori criterion to hold citizenship and law and society will function according to the logic of multiplicity.

b) A transnational web of queer bridges overcomes national boundaries, enabling the creation of a global politics in diversity. The idea of *nepantla*, "a liminal zone" or "a constant state of displacement" (Anzaldúa 2002b: 1) transforms the function of bridges: they are no longer just crossing ways; they are determinant in the incessant process of forging bonds across race, gender, and alternative identity lines (Anzaldúa 2002a: 574). This proposal of perpetual crossing offers an alternative view of globalization.

c) Since segregating practices occur as a result of gender and ethnic asymmetry (i.e., heterosexual vs. homosexual, white vs. Amerindian, etc.), the study of such oppression must question ethnic and gender assumptions. This is the point of departure for a project that goes beyond these categories. Rather than treating ethnicity or gender as a grounding upon which to understand subjectivity, Anzaldúa's view teaches us to depart from the body when reflecting on the experiences that define the self, and, from there, to reconnect with various people in order to build a commonality based on diversity called "el mundo zurdo" (Anzaldúa 2015: 209). One of Anzaldúa's dearest causes is the need to resignify differences as a starting point for constructing inclusive communities.

The principle of queering consists of opening up an antihegemonic space for the excluded, oppressed, and disenfranchised individuals; their exclusion is multiple, as they are excluded from colonial institutions as well as from subaltern communities. Latin American subalternist and decolonial scholars have not paid much attention to sexual diversity, except for a few mentions in their listings of the groups excluded by hegemonic society. Anzaldúa's nonhegemonic sexualities and Rivera Cusicanqui's (2010) subaltern queer of the third republic share a similar cultural location— in the liminal and illegitimate zone reserved for those excluded and lacking of full citizenship. In some cases they might have a relative cultural legitimization, such as in the Zapotec example, but, even though they enjoy a form of tolerance, sexual difference remains invisible in the dominant mestizo discourse. The Chilean writer Pedro Lemebel (2000) also pointed out the characteristic double exclusion of the queer in his celebrated poem "Hablo por mi diferencia," in which he noted the marginalization of sexual difference even in the community of dissident activists in post-dictatorial Chile, revealing a reproduction of oppression among

the various ranks of sex–gender categories within social groups
(93–97).

Conclusion

To conclude this chapter, I would like to make three observations.
First, queerness does not predate the colonial order; instead, it
should be seen as an unexpected result of colonial oppression.
This does not mean that nonheterosexual practices were absent in
pre-Columbian cultures but rather that they were not condemned
or deemed to be deviant. Colonialism's internal contradictions
are made manifest within queerness itself, and, as a result, queer
subjects are able to develop visceral forms of resistance to power,
a type of bodily rejection of colonial law. In this sense, the
visceral archive as conceived of by Tortorici (2014) is a catalog
of transgressive reactions to colonial biopolitics. Pre-Columbian
sexual practices should not be seen as transgression to any sex–
gender norms within specific pre-Columbian societies; rather,
the sexual practices of pre-Columbian societies were only deemed
nefarious and grave violations of God's law by colonial powers, and
at this point became causes for prosecution.

Second, decolonizing is not a question of re-establishing a pre-
Columbian sex–gender system; rather, it should be conceived as a
restructuring of the forms of citizenship produced inside coloniality.
Recovering the ancestral is a utopian desire that functions as an
imaginary resource sometimes helpful in narrating decolonizing
struggles. The ways that Garza Carvajal (2003), Horswell (2005),
Sigal (2007), and Tortorici (2014) revisit and reconceive the
colonial archive are illustrative of a type of archeological search
for textual fragments dealing with the politics of the body and
the uses and meanings of sexuality. This method of historicizing
sexuality uncovers the processes of the criminalization, discipline,
and punishment of sexual diversity. The search for an ancestral

sexuality within the archive may give us some fragmentary pieces of valuable information about dismantled systems of belief and worldviews, but these bits will always be read or translated through the distorting filter of ideologies and discourses. The process of decolonizing sexuality in a colonial text requires a type of deep reflection on the nature of translation, liberating the text from Western misreadings.

Third, not simply a nostalgic celebration of the archeology of queerness, the history of Latin American sexuality reveals the process of colonization to be based on a politics of the body. As colonialism is understood, its webs of control can begin to be untangled. It can be said that the use of the native in political and academic discourses is another form of translating the colonized, in this case for the express purpose of making the bodies of the colonized readable to Western epistemologies (i.e., the formation of a coloniality of knowledge). The study of the coloniality of sex would be a project of knowing how bodies are used as part of a colonial program of domination. A decolonization of sex would be, then, a process of redefining the norms of the bodies in question; such a process would require the liberation of sexual practices from the limits of colonial law, which has heretofore restricted sexuality and gender to a binary configuration reflecting Western misogynistic and homophobic biases. Then, we need to conceive of decolonization as a dismantling of colonial norms. Although these norms may be articulated in the doctrine of the colonizing church (as well as in other places), they cannot be derogated just by deleting the text of the law but by a systematic dismantling of the ideology introjected into the lives of the colonized subject. Subject formation according to the strict guidelines of colonial rule is the basic method of colonial domination.

CHAPTER 2

Queerness and the nation in peripheral modernity

Queer coloniality analyses show us that queerness cannot be defined by itself; rather, it must be defined in relation to a set frame of reference according to which something is considered queer. In the colonial period, that point of reference was the Spanish law against nefarious sin. As in most parts of social life and culture, Latin American sexuality and gender are framed within the order established during the colonial period; the legacy of this colonial order still structures the forms of domination and social hierarchies we see today. For Rita Segato (2011), colonial gender relations are reproduced and crystalized into a permanent form in the modern republican state (17). Dominant discourses sustain the definition of Latin American sexuality through a system of differences and exclusions; throughout history these discourses have articulated a variety of narratives and representations that have recolonized the body under renewed terms. In the age of Spanish domination, queerness was a theological rationale for punishing and killing the sexual deviant; for the liberal state established after independence in the nineteenth century, that divine reference continues to determine the sex–gender system of surveillance although the religious discourse is not openly manifested. Instead, other discourses (such as the national, the medical, and the criminological) become the points of reference when implementing public policies that marginalize what religious ideology has deemed deviant since the time of the conquest. The mechanisms of exclusion set up by colonization are now reinforced by new dominant discourses, in which the concept of combating sin has evolved into a modern concept of social cleansing and public hygiene; in effect, the Christian principle is now sustained on a unconscious level. The history of modernization informs what Latin American thinkers call neocolonialism and internal colonialism (two of the main conceptual proposals of the twentieth century for understanding Latin American society), in which the line of exclusion is articulated through behavioral and criminal sciences; these discursive fields serve to keep the ideology of national identity as the main criterion in defining admissible and nonadmissible bodily practices. While for the colonial period queerness was located in the body of the native, for the independent states, queerness will be located in the Europeanized and the antinational elite. In this chapter, my aim is to review the discourses of sexual exclusion in modern Latin America: principally, the articulation of national identity and the modern apparatus of exclusion (namely criminalization and medicalization) work in concert to name and acknowledge sexual diversity while presenting it as the zone of the repudiable.

Since the 1980s, a rich corpus of scholarship has dealt with defining the discourses, politics, and social practices that specify Latin American sex–gender marginalities. My argument is that this academic conversation focuses not only on the marginal (the lines that demarcate the cultural, conceptual, cognitive, and physical borders of gender and sexuality) but also on the concealed, the disguised, and the suggested forms of queerness within cultural practices deemed prestigious in national cultural traditions. Queer studies' main object of inquiry—as introduced in the Latin Americanist academic forums—includes nonconventional sexualities and nonnormative gender expressions. Their representation in literature and the arts and their inclusion in criminal and medical archives are the main materials of analysis of queer scholarship. Deconstruction, performance studies, post-Lacanian and post-Foucauldian approaches, the studies of the national and postnational, and postcolonial and decolonial perspectives are some of the conceptual sources that have nurtured thought on sexual diversity and gender heterodoxies.

Since the times of colonization, queerness has existed within the public sphere as a trope of insult, a violent speech act, as Federico Garza Carvajal (2003) argues, used to consolidate the *vir*, the masculinity of the conqueror, whose maleness itself provided the Spaniards with a sense of superiority. The *vir* functions as an imperialistic myth that deems sodomite and nefarious all the conquered others, feminizing them while assigning the colonizer himself the status of the antonomasia of Catholicism and heterosexuality. This differentiation underlines the uneven relationship between colonizer and colonized that Aníbal Quijano points out as one of the axes of coloniality (the other one being the labor exploitation of the non-European) (Quijano 2000: 533). The political use of the condemnation of all other sexualities is then rooted in the very foundational narratives of Latin America. The conqueror's *vir*, which feminized the indigenous as a method of colonization (as a symbolic mark of dominion), did not disappear in the republican period inaugurated by the independence movements of the nineteenth century. The independent society provides the creole and the mestizo—the prototype of the national man—the privilege of the *vir* as a political device to combat the stranger to the nation and the enemy of the people. Two paradigmatic cases can be considered foundational narratives of feminization as a political metaphor for the disempowering of the Europeanized elite in favor of the national *vir*: the Argentinean short story "El matadero" by Esteban Echeverría about 1830s Buenos Aires, and the scandal of the Baile de los 41 (Ball of the 41), in Mexico City in 1901.

In terms of queerness in Latin America, modernity implies a consolidation of society's abject, a reduction of diversity to the universal pretensions of Western civilization through juridical discipline, objectification, and disenfranchisement. A queer critique of modernity centers around an analysis of medical and juridical discipline and shows that sexual diversity is excluded from representations of national identity as it is deemed criminal and pathological. It is in these exclusionary processes of naming the abject that the construction of dissident sexual identities originates. Still, despite modernity's relentless processes of exclusion, Latin American cultural production continues to be a place where queerness emerges as an aesthetic feature and a form of unavoidable desire that is consistently present in—and often central to—modern literature and the arts. It is this tension that defines queerness in modernity, the main subject of this chapter.

The modern politics of the body

In Latin America, modern nationalism is the synthesis of two forms of anxiety: first, the modern imperative for the nation-state to always be seen as in good standing—and ultimately as "civilized"—within a historical model based on continuous progress; and second, the need to present the nation (through a variety of educative and propagandistic strategies) as the mythic form under which many symbolic commonalities might be unified. We will see that these two imperatives contradict one another. The contradictions inherent in the nationalistic program come to light especially when we consider how the nation accommodates (or does not accommodate) queer subjects. On the one hand, the modern state apparatus is an instrument used to discipline and exclude queer subjects, and, on the other hand, "queerness" is a constant source of innovation (hence, of modernization) in many different aspects of social life, in the arts, and in ways of living and thinking. In the keynote panel of the conference Queering Paradigms (in February 2014, in Quito, Ecuador), political scientist Nikita Dhawan (2016) suggested this contradiction when she defined modernity and queerness through the Derridean conceptualization of the Platonic concept of *pharmakon*, the substance with the paradoxical capacity to heal and destroy at the same time. Queerness is conceived of in contradictory terms—both as a contaminating agent (or a pathogen element such as a virus or bacteria) and as a contributing factor in the progressive modernization of the nation-state.

As in the aforementioned work of Zeb Tortorici (2014) describing the colonial locus of queerness, the criminal archive is one of the main sources through which to make a discursive evaluation of deviant sexuality in Latin American modernity. Tortorici's detailed evaluation of the archive explains the process by which those sexual "unnameable" practices became, finally, to be named. For Carlos Monsiváis (2003), the enunciation moment, and then visibility, of same-sex desire in Mexico was the scandal of the so-called Ball of the 41 in 1901, a private party of transvestite upper-class men that was amply publicized in the Mexican press. By means of criminalization and public scorn, the unnamed desire was displayed for the public scrutiny. It is through scandal, the product of mass media and of governmental and public attention, that the silence about the unspeakable sin is broken (Monsiváis 2003: 150). The centenary of this event was celebrated with a transnational conference at Tulane University in November 2001. The anthology resulting from this conference, *The Famous 41*, edited by Robert McKee Irwin, Edward J. McCaughan, and Michelle Rocio Nasser (2003), gathers together a number of essays devoted to studying the conditions of enunciation of difference in the context of the Porfirian belle époque (1876–1911).

Queerness became visible at the moment of its very first intense public condemnation. All images related to queerness were received as repudiable; queer images could then be used as types of weapons to denigrate enemies. In his essay "Homophobia and the Mexican Working Class, 1900–1910," historian Robert Buffington (2003) explains that queerness had a political function in Mexican newspaper cartoons of the time. Cross-dressing was used to devalue someone's political character; coding an enemy with "effeminacy" had the power to debilitate him/her. For Buffington (2003), cross-dressing's displacement here—from the field of derogatory exposure of actual feminized men to the field of satirical representations of political enemies—has no relation to homophobic expression as political enemies who were cross-dressed were not exposed as homosexuals but as weak, vain, or inconsistent, traits that are "metaphoric connections with the feminine" (199). Still, I would argue that homophobia was strongly evoked in the press' strategy of using cross-dressing to devalue men by dispossessing them of their masculinity (or *vir*), showing that the vices criticized in the cartoons were as repudiable as effeminacy: the abominable sin persisted as a means to exercise symbolic violence, even though the targeted individual was not known as a feminine man. In this way, effeminacy is itself considered an insult; it functions as a political weapon, tactically deployed through a process of codifying cross-dressing as a sign of weakness, cowardice, and treason. Following that logic, the public scorn of the upper-class, cross-dressed men in the Ball of the 41 (it is rumored that President Porfirio Díaz's son-in-law was among them) provided the perfect verification of the decadence of the Porfirian elite at large. After the revolution of 1910 defeated this dictatorship, the usage of queerness as a way of disempowering the oligarchy would be, in consequence, one of the discursive components of gender ideology in the postrevolutionary state.

Previously, queerness as a political discourse used to disempower enemies was present in the period of the formation of the Argentine nation. In his *Médicos, maleantes y maricas*, the Argentine historian Jorge Salessi (1995) references how traditional interpretations of Esteban Echeverría's canonical nineteenth-century short story "El matadero" treat it as an allegory of barbarism's rape of civilization (Salessi 1995: 63). The masculine character raped by the slaughterhouse's crowd is identified as the *unitario*, which, within the allegory, represents a political position (effectively endorsed by Echeverría) that favors Europeanization of the country. This well-educated and refined man, who embodies a modern Western civilization, is the victim of torture and rape by the nationalistic (described as barbarian) *rosistas*, the followers of the dictator Juan Manuel de Rosas. Traditional, creole nationalism, represented by Rosas' crowd of followers in the story, repudiates modern nationalism, represented by the educated cosmopolitan *unitario*.

Nevertheless, the criticism of the barbarian—embodied by the mestizo, black, and indigenous population—by the urban Europeanized elite did not prevent nineteenth-century Argentine literature from being fascinated with the gaucho (the countryside mestizo man) to the point of creating an entire poetic genre around this vernacular character: *la gauchesca*, in which we can observe the construction of an emblematic masculine figure that contains all the features of virility that would come to define the national. Even though the Europeanized elite controlled the country, Argentine nationalism was best represented throughout the nineteenth century by the figure of the gaucho, the typifying supporter of Rosas. The Spanish *vir*, then, was replaced by the national *vir*, and homophobia was one of the era's underlining features. The limits of heterosexuality were also the limits of nationality. In "El matadero," national ideology deems the modern character, the *unitario*, to be effeminate for being a Westernizer, then presented as antinational.

Sexual difference is then read as a Western contamination of the Rosas' followers. As in the case of the Mexican political caricatures, queerness is assigned to political enemies, and anyone presumed to lack virility does not add value to the collective national character.

Within the logic of Echeverría's Argentinean story and the Mexican Ball of the 41, proscribing the queer subject keeps the nation healthy and prevents society from decay. A positivist ideology, which relies on biological principles to understand social and cultural phenomena, helped to keep heterosexuality as the defining core of nation in nineteenth century Latin American political discourse. Modernity applies its instruments of control against sexual deviants with the objective of keeping the nation safe from queer contamination. Salessi's (1995) historiography centers around the mechanisms of disciplining bodies in nineteenth- and twentieth-century Argentina, the period of the establishment of a liberal and modern state. In public discourse, hygiene becomes a constant rhetorical figure, one that aligns biological and criminological inquiries in order to diagnose as a health issue whatever is considered immoral in the Catholic ideology. Nationalism is modern, Salessi (1995) points out, "for being a product of an inductive process that used scientific methods in an environment like the school, conceived as an especially apt place for a sociological manipulation in that formative moment of modern Argentina" (222, my translation). When we see how often science is used as a social ordering tool to consolidate a national identity, it becomes clear what the liberal conception of the modern state actually is: the modern state translates discourses mainly from Western centers of knowledge production into local variants that serve the express purpose of continuing the colonial past's system of exclusion (though now, couched in the terms of national identity). Based on this modern process, by which a national conscience is determined, it is possible to argue that, regarding sex and gender, nationality is a disguised form of the same colonial exclusionary system. In the modernization process of Latin American countries, scientific discourse became an instrument for reinforcing the uneven relationships characterizing the colonial system (Quijano 2000: 533).

Scientific discourse on sexuality functions as an ideological apparatus that has intervened in political struggles in various regions of the continent. For example, amid the turmoil of Cuban independence, scientific discourse once again intervened by excluding the queer body from the national ideology, aiming to expel the Spanish colonizers. In his reading of the controversy unleashed after the publication in 1888 of *La prostitución de la ciudad de la Habana* (Havana City's Prostitution) by the Cuban physician Benjamín de Céspedes, Wilfredo Hernández (2006) observes how treating homosexuality as a medical category played an important role in the ideology of Cuban independence. Céspedes attributes the spreading of homosexual "disease" to the Spanish immigrants. The intellectuals who favored Spanish domination of the island reacted immediately to Céspedes' accusation, denouncing his lack of professionalism in introducing this supposed public health diagnosis into the debates between those in favor of independence and the colonialist politicians. Scientific discourse became a rough part of the political debate. As a result, the terms of the political dialogue changed: the political positions were now evaluated in terms of their truth values, how they were constructed, and how scientifically valid they were according to the normativities that drew on the contemporary state of knowledge production. Hernández notes that the main respondent to Céspedes' theses, P. Giralt, corrected what he saw to be Céspedes' main confusion— conflating prostitution, which is motivated by economic need, with pederasty (motivated by vice) (Hernández 2006: 36–37). When Giralt disentangled Céspedes' perceived mistake, the culpability was reversed (in what turned out to be a politically convenient way for his pro-Spain cause). For Céspedes, the medically ill partner in the relationship was the passive "pederast" (according to the terminology of the time)—the subservient position in homoerotic intercourse, the one who offers sexual service and (importantly for Céspedes' political motivations) usually a Spanish immigrant. Giralt countered the political argument by reversing the culpability: in his view, it was the client—the top position, who was purportedly looking for sex not for any "medical" need but for pure vice—who should be considered ill.

In 1928, another debate over the national cleansing of the ills of queerness emerged on the island. Cuban journalists Sergio Carbó and Mariblanca Sabas Alomá undertook a campaign against the *pepillinos* and *garzonas*,[1] two types of people considered deviant with respect to Cuba's heteronormative creole norms. The *pepillinos* and *garzonas* were accused of embracing American culture in their appearance and corporeal practices. *Pepillinos* were depicted with mannerisms and in elegant attire, and *garzonas* with looseness and a lack of prudery (Sierra Madero 2006: 81–82). The caricatures and sardonic comments published in the magazines *La semana* and *Carteles* open up a nationalistic division between the national body and the colonized queered one. As in the Argentine case of *rosistas* and *unitarios*, and the cases of Cuban independence and the Mexican revolution, the queered body once again functioned as an image for depicting political rivals pejoratively.

The relationship between queerness and the modern nation is also legible in the urban landscape of the modern city. In *Beyond Carnival: Male Sexuality in Twentieth-Century Brazil*, American historian James N. Green (1999) looks at gay culture in Brazil. His analysis works as both an architectonic and a physiological history: he maps the cities Rio de Janeiro and São Paulo by situating a history of the visibility of homosexuality in those places. As criticism

---

[1] Pejorative names that designate effeminate men and masculinized women, respectively.

has focused increasingly on the performative, most academic work on queer culture in Latin America has considered visuality to be among the most important terrains for analysis. A methodology of visuality consists of depicting and decoding pictorial documents, or reflecting on visibility as a central matter for the construction of queer subjectivities. This very visibility—appearance, appearing, or the process of becoming seen—performs the appropriation of public spaces by sex–gender dissidents. Homosexuals resignify the cartography of the city and install themselves in the urban landscape by disruption. With a broad, well-investigated sampling of research, *Beyond Carnival* allows us not only to appreciate the determinant influence of homoerotic culture in Brazil—an irrefutable statement in the wake of Green's exhaustive historiographical work—but also to underline the emergence of a politics that is articulated beyond logocentric strategies, in the terrain of the body itself.

Throughout Green's (1999) book, we can see how queer visibility and law are in a process of continuous negotiation. Illness and crime are the main excuses and rationales given for the way the state (through its associated apparatuses) stigmatizes queer bodies, ostracizing them and making them invisible in the public sphere. Case studies based on judiciary and clinical documents show a pattern in the way homosexual men coped with the law and its unforgiving punishments throughout the majority of the twentieth century in Brazil. The options for homosexual men proved to be somewhat limited: most migrated from the countryside to the city; there, some were involved in male prostitution activities, while others simply took advantage of certain spaces conducive to cruising in order to find sexual partners. For example, these men were allowed during carnival festivities to openly cross-dress and roam the streets without police harassment. Outside the carnival, they developed strategies to avoid persecution while cruising public spaces. Toleration during carnival allowed gays to stage their masquerade for the public to see, but they had to flee persecution during the rest of the year. While this co-optive relationship might be described as a fluctuating dynamic of tolerance and exclusion, it ended up leading to the establishment of a vibrant queer culture that nourishes one of the emblematic symbols of national identity: the carnival.

Green (1999) vividly portrays the process by which the intervention of queerness has been fundamental in the construction of Brazil's national culture. In its wavering opinions about queer culture—from a staunch disapproval to a final embrace of the social theatrical event of the carnival (protagonized by queer performers)—the national heteronormative regime reveals its fundamental contradictions. The contradictory treatment of queer culture should indeed be interpreted as a crisis of the modern state, if not as an ulterior consequence of modernity itself. At the very least, Green's work reveals the internal paradoxes of the patriarchal state: the state was itself made queer as it tried to expel what it had named queer. In the very act of naming what is not desirable to the dominant ideology, its desire is proclaimed. Covering the shame of effeminacy has the ultimate consequence of turning the effeminate body into the true focal point in the proscenium of the nation; we can see this process happen by means of a type of aesthetic seduction, as analyzed in the following pages.

The aesthetic weapon of queerness

If gender and sexual dissidence is deemed antinational, homophobia has to be reinforced in order to keep the national body safe from queer contamination and, in turn, homophobia must be considered a part of public policy. *Gay Cuban Nation* by Emilio Bejel (2001) focuses on the continuous recomposition of the Cuban national identity via the country's repeated attempts to proscribe alternative sexualities. The book's chronological structure lets us follow the transformation of the nation in relation to its various interpretations of the non-normative body. It underlines the notion that national identity is based on heteronormative discourse. When homosexuality is excluded from the national norm, the very contours of homosexual practice are drawn; in this way, homosexuality is the negative projection of the national self. Homosexuality is rejected as illness and vice, but the very exhibition of the state's rejection becomes the screen that allows for the visibility of a gay cultural underground. The rationale for this exclusion is familiar; the heteronormative state uses medical knowledge to keep homosexuality at the margin of the national project. As seen in many of the cases we have reviewed in this chapter, medical, scientific discourse determines a national hegemonic politics centered around sex–gender policy. Despite Cuba's insistence on its staunch disapproval of queer culture in all its guises, *Gay Cuban Nation*'s reading of prominent Cuban authors, criminologists, and sexologists demonstrates the role of homosexual visibility in the formation of the nation. Although the integrity of the nation and the hygiene of society impose a homophobic norm and an exclusionary medical practice, Bejel's survey shows that homoeroticism must be included in the inventory of the national; on its face, we cannot deny the fact that the category of rejected bodies and prosecuted sexual and cultural practices is a significant part of Cuba's literature and other discourses, such as medicine and criminology.

One of Bejel's (2001) most interesting propositions consists of opposing the medicalization and criminalization of sexual difference—that is, the positivist discourses that disciplined the queer body—to aesthetic representations of queerness. Aesthetic values proved to be the bases for the decriminalization of sexual difference and the ultimate disavowal of the medical and psychological diagnosis of homosexuality as a disease. Thus, José Lezama Lima (1977), one of the most influential Cuban authors of the twentieth century, proposed going beyond the limits imposed by the positivist assumptions, by presenting the homoerotic as associated with spiritual values. While scientific and criminal treatises revealed the presence of the homosexual body as an opposite to the national gender prescription, literature paved the way for the inclusion of queer subjects in society as prominent citizens and respectable members of the "lettered city."[2] I must stress that this does not simply mean that scientific and literary discourses are opposed. Homosexuality and the construction of the national imaginary are related in many contradictory ways. While homosexuals are forced to hide their sexual orientation, implicit— and explicit enough—queer narratives and images circulate in the cultural environment. Bejel's book is a historical account of homosexuality as it relates to the national program in Cuba; he stresses those elements of homosexual culture that destabilize the heterosexual assumption of the national. Heterosexuality and homosexuality are imagined entities, but they have very real cultural impacts as they are the notions that define and control bodies (and the same might be said of the nation—an imaginary with various tangible apparatuses of social control). The Cuban state's politics regarding different bodies (and its corollaries—the identity politics of difference set off against the state's hegemony) are, then, the main focus of Bejel's criticism. His method consists of evaluating the discourses that discipline and exclude difference, but also the ones that deem difference desirable.

Queerness has become a mark of modernity in the Latin American elite by overcoming the criterion of mere sexual difference. In his essay "The *Lagartijo* at *The High Life*: Masculine Construction, Race, Nation, and Homosexuality in Porfirian Mexico," compiled in the volume *The Famous 41*, Víctor Macías-González (2003) depicts the culture of consumption of upper-class males of the Porfiriato

---

[2] I use this term to refer to what Uruguayan intellectual Ángel Rama (1998) conceived as the lettered class, which has an influence on public decisions: writers, artists, and public intellectuals are included in this Latin American elite (21).

linking queerness to the privileges associated with being modern. In this work, the modern man is depicted as being an expert in the latest trends of sumptuous goods, to the point that he is deemed a savvy arbiter of the elite's way of life. Macías-González terms this contradiction as follows: "in the consumption practices that proclaimed elite males' patriotism and modernity, as well as their class and racial superiority, also lurked the sinister specter of moral danger, for the devotion of dandies' time as resources to conspicuous consumption perilously mimicked what society considered a strictly feminine behavior" (232). While presumed modern and patriotic, upper-class males in the Porfirian era were also obsessed with consumption, which ended up leaving them afflicted with a not-so-virile physiological constitution. By virtue of their conspicuous consumption, the descendants of the colonizer stratum—meaning the creole elite—added to their stereotyped reputation: this class of people's unproductive, superfluous "European" features marked them as feminine, which was interpreted as a sign of the decadence of the regime, a prominent failure to perform the *vir*, the manly energy that once made colonization (as well as the national independence struggles) possible.

For Robert Buffington (2003), the Ball of the 41 scandal can be interpreted as the deployment of what he terms as "harbingers of false modernity," in reference to the *jotos* (faggots) of the upper classes in Porfirian Mexico (201). That perception was disseminated in the penny press of the period, which allows Buffington to assert that working-class homophobia in the Mexico of the period "functioned as a powerful subversive tool capable of undermining the ideological foundation of the bourgeois authority grounded in heteronormative and nuclear family values" (220–221). Homophobia works by tracing a line of exclusion, rejecting all that is not heterosexual and national (under the patriarchal Christian rule); through this distinction, homophobia is able to preserve the hegemony of a heterosexual masculine subjectivity, on which the very definition of the national rests. Nevertheless, Macías-González (2003) argues that the imperative of modernizing the nation places hegemonic masculinity at the very edge of queerness. The crisis of the whole system of gender that the modern contradiction between heterosexual and homosexual has unleashed in Western civilization, according to Sedgwick (1990), has found in Latin American societies an additional twist: the paradoxical relation between the national and the modern regarding gender ideology (1). It is on the basis of this paradox that significant scholarship has been produced; I would like to group these scholars' efforts under the term *queering the nation*. Queering the nation involves finding the internal contradictions of those modern, national ideologies that constantly evade their own gender assumptions; these fundamental contradictions produce an instability in the very realms of bodily practices and institutional control of bodies (understood in Foucauldian terms as biopolitics).

Queerness has been seen as an anxiety of modern consumption (as we have seen in the scholarly work of Macías-González 2003). This line of thought implies a certain type of queer aesthetics, one in which the decorative and the exquisite are considered good taste; at its most extreme, a queer aesthetic here could be reduced to a residual ornament of the privileged. The prevalent literary and artistic movement at the turn of the twentieth century—called *modernismo*[3]—was obsessed with aestheticism, mysticism, and sentimental brotherhood. The emphasis on sentimentality, according to literary critic Sylvia Molloy (2003), makes the Mexican *modernista* Amado Nervo's poetry a place where the poet feminizes himself but then establishes sentimental brotherhood

---

[3] I will use the terms *modernismo* and *modernista* in Spanish to refer to the turn-of-the-twentieth-century literary Latin American and Spanish style, strongly influenced by the *fin de siècle* European symbolist and decadent aesthetics. Using these terms in Spanish helps us to distinguish this aesthetic current from the twentieth-century aesthetic called *modernism* in Anglo-Saxon culture.

with men (300). Several pieces of queer criticism have focused on *modernismo*'s aesthetics, a style in which queerness is often present: the exotic, the extraordinary, the excessive, and the monstrous are always held up as its primary characteristics. Critic Oscar Montero's (1993, 1998) readings of the poets and essayists Julián del Casal (Cuban), José Enrique Rodó (Uruguayan), and Rubén Darío (Nicaraguan) as well as Alfredo Villanueva-Collado's (1996) critical analysis of still other authors Augusto d'Halmar (Chilean) and José Asunción Silva (Colombian) show how sensuality and the strange lend a sensibility of queerness to the artistic representations grouped under the term *modernismo*.

The case of the Chilean novelist Augusto d'Halmar and his artistic community Colonia Tolstoiana (Tolstoian Colony) is one of those experiments that disguised homoeroticism as an aesthetic project filled with symbolist rhetoric; in typical *modernista* fashion, the cultivation of an alternative lifestyle is deemed an artistic enterprise. In his *Memorias de un tolsotiano* (A Tolstoian's Memories) (1955), Fernando Santiván details the norms this community observed, among them a prohibition on admitting women into their group. This book is able to tell the truth but only in terms of what is speakable within its epistemic horizon (the social/literary context that determines the discursive enunciations available to the author). Santiván's book is an example of a text that brushes up against its own limits. We have to keep this limitation in mind in order to read the moments that function as a type of ellipsis—the gaps in the text that refer to same-sex attraction. The ellipses should not be explained as simply a fear of talking about what is forbidden; instead they originate in the problem of not having a discursive instrument to represent the homoerotic that is approved by the addressed community of readers. However, this book shows traces of a hidden motive (the homoerotic aspect of Colonia Tolstoiana) via its frequent allusions to d'Halmar's mysterious disease—allusions which disguise the moral pain of being in the closet. That is to say, sexuality has left its traces on the writing in the form of a discourse about pathology. In light of the limitations of the text's discursive horizon, sexuality (while nonexistent explicitly) can be seen to be presented through implication, as a negative space, and the text is organized around those gaps. Finding these traces reveals not only what is unspoken but also how the art of secrecy as a literary project is articulated. Oscar Montero's (1998) reading of the story of Hilas in *Motivos de Proteo* (The Motives of Proteus) by José Enrique Rodó points out the empty center covered by secrecy (167): in *modernismo*, the lack of reference to the body is one of the most frequent rhetorical strategies used to refer to homoerotic desire through silence. What really is covered by the gesture of secrecy is the empty trace of the repressed. The gesture of aestheticism is, then, pointing out the place where the repressed was.

Santiván's (1955) narrative builds on the secret of a social transgression that has a limited space in which to exist. Despite the rules of decorum, the space of the body has a metastatic effect in culture at large: the distortion invades other aspects of life, condemning all areas where "transgression" is represented, rendering it as a perverted zone, a space of infection within a general social life. Decorum—that is, the rhetorical strategies through which sexual content is indirectly named—is not enough to cover and dissimulate the morbid implications of same-sex attraction. A double difficulty is experienced in *Memorias de un tolsotiano*: on the one hand, Santiván has to implement the strategies of decorum used by *modernistas* to conceal heterosexual sex in a biography that is more accurately about homosexual desire; on the other hand, he has to disclose the morbid nature of his problematic relationship with d'Halmar without being explicit about d'Halmar's "disease." The task of this writing is to occlude sex and disease from the reader's eyes, but traces of these elements still appear. Decorum is one of the stylistic topics that has been discussed since the first readings of the book. In a note published in the Chilean newspaper *El Mercurio*, in 1955, Ricardo Latchman, for instance, argued that, "despite the general realism, a poetic tone, an evocative remark of enormous fineness attenuates what is scabrous and avoids always what in less expert hands would become an explosive and offensive substance" (quoted in Tzitsikos 1985: 202, my translation). The "offensive substance" that is avoided in Santiván's (1955) writing is obscenity (thus hiding the scandalous and disguising anything that might be contrary to prudish sensibilities). Still, this contemporaneous review shows that Latchman, like many readers of his time, could see the scabrous and could decode the discursive web: though there is not precisely a preoccupation with hidden matter, there is a code through which the censored obscene is presented. Traces are also readable signs. Santiván's confession shows the scars of the sick body as supplementary signs that lead the reader to recognize the secrecy. Here, I agree with José Quiroga (1999) words: "The homosexual remains precisely in a trace, in a track, that barely reaches the surface so as to be consigned again to the supplementary" (viii).

Uncovering the traces of queerness is the method that Daniel Balderston (2000) applies to his reading of Argentinean writer Jorge Luis Borges' fictions and essays. Thus, the traces of homoerotic desire are found in the ellipses and the most mysterious moments of his narrative. For instance, in his reading of the short story "La secta del fénix" (The Phoenix's Sect), Balderston sees those traces in the description of a secret shared among a diversity of people, all of whom are complicit and keep the secret. The secret that Borges never reveals, according to Balderston (2000), is masculine homosexuality (70–71). Even though it is true that Borges never refers explicitly to homoerotic desire, the critic is able to read silence and mystery themselves as marks of queerness.

In the introduction to his gay and lesbian Chilean literature compilation *A corazón abierto: Geografía literaria de la homosexualidad en Chile* (In Open Heart: Literary Geography of Chilean Homosexuality), Juan Pablo Sutherland (2001) asserts that the homosexual history of Chile is not in the main narratives but in the corners of supplementary, minor narratives—texts found in places such as Chile's oral tradition and yellow journalism (14). The great narratives ignore sexual diversity entirely. Codes of decorum are intended to hide the sexualized body; therefore, homosexuality must be reserved to the private space. As a private issue, homosexuality is still shameful. Nevertheless, the intellectual's life and the artist's life became objects of curiosity for a generation of Latin Americanists studying sexual diversity in the 1980s and 1990s. They applied close readings of literary and personal writings, developing deconstructive and psychoanalytical analyses of canonical figures of the letters and public life. Such are the works by Daniel Balderston (1998, 2000), Licia Fiol-Matta (2002), Oscar Montero (1993, 1998), and Sylvia Molloy (1991, 2003), to name a few. But unearthing the intimacy of the lettered elite has remained controversial in the twenty-first century. Any publication that refers to Chilean Nobel Prize winner Gabriela Mistral's lesbianism, for instance, has received heated reactions in Chile (see, for example, Rivas San Martín 2012).

The question that arises concerns the intended audience of *modernista* writing and its recent scholarship: are these studies aimed at a particular elitist counterculture that, with its admittance in the lettered city, can decode a complex rhetorical game of ambiguities and readable silences? Or do they aim to problematize the sex–gender structure at large (much in the same way that Sedgwick (1990) understands so-called minority issues to be universal)? The exploration of the concealed in mainstream literary production has been one of the main tasks queer scholarship has undertaken since the 1980s. In the history of Latin American culture, homosexuality has been a problematic topic regarding the biographies of prominent writers and intellectuals such as Mário de Andrade, José Lezama

Lima, Gabriela Mistral, and Xavier Villaurrutia, whose works hold canonical stature, despite their authors' reputation of living outside heteronormative mores. In fact, each of these authors lived in a more or less transparent form of closet. This ambiguity of the Latin American closet means that sexual difference exists in a type of liminal space between the private and public spheres. For the literary critic Sylvia Molloy (1991), autobiography can acquire social value when the self is linked to communitarian and public affairs (20–21). The private gets made public when it is of interest to the public. While most autobiographical writing inscribes the public in the private (a self-conscious display of a private life for the world to see), the writing of the sexual dissident operates in reverse: as we have seen in the case of the *modernista* authors, the private is inscribed in public texts. This process of inscription is what characterizes queer writing in Latin America. In this way, we can say that queer literature's construction of visible silences introduces sexual difference into the public arena. It is in that inscription that the queering of the public space is happening. The description of rhetorical mechanisms and discursive instability caused by this queering has been one of the most noticeable academic discussions regarding sexual and gender dissidence.

In his prologue to the volume *Mapa callejero: Crónicas sobre lo gay en América Latina* (Street Map: Chronicles on Gayness in Latin America), José Quiroga (2010) observes that texts about the culture of cruising in public spaces have created a new form of knowledge of the city: the city's cartography is an erotic web of connections between men in coffee shops, on streets, and on corners. The *crónica* (which, in English, might be translated as "chronicle") is a very specific genre within Latin American letters, a type of writing about the modern city that straddles the line between nonfiction and fiction and that was popularized in the late nineteenth and early twentieth centuries. More particularly, these gay chronicles should be seen as a genre that is typified by the way they feature an estrangement of the urban order (Quiroga 2010: 12–13). Quiroga's study focuses on a particular genre of writing: to narrate daily transgressions of heterosexual norms, many narratives since the end of the nineteenth century have discussed how public spaces have been the sites of homoerotic flirting and sexual trade. The chronicle, that literary nonfictional form located somewhere between journalistic reportage and the short story, became a device for inscribing sexual dissidence in the public sphere. This inscription is always mediated by the rhetorical codes of euphemism: through suggestive allusions readable only for the initiated, the authors of chronicles can introduce homoerotic desire into a public text while also satisfying editorial policies (which are evidenced by the strategic condemnations and moral lessons that often feature within these queer writings).

The chronicle (*crónica*) often contends with the limits of censorship, and these texts constantly rub up against the codes of prudery. Homosexuals intervene in various areas of social life while their sexuality must be kept a private, unmentioned aspect of their life. The morality of what is visible in the public is framed within these texts as a question of social protocol and good manners. Still, the key to these texts is that they never entirely avoid references to that which breaks the norms of sexual morality. For the chronicle writer, it is more honorable and distinguished to include allusions to the sexually illicit by skillfully and artfully disguising them with rhetorical strategies that keep the entire narration completely wrapped up in the veil of discretion. The art of discretion remains one of the most valued abilities of the honorable gentile class— along with prudence, reservation, and diplomacy. Veiled references to unsanctioned sexual practices are what is required to meet the norms of this distinguished society. Ultimately, it is the very art of discretion that fosters the formation of an elite subculture of queer intimacy. Public figures, intellectuals, artists, and entrepreneurs are expected to observe the norms of discretion, which tacitly constructs a comfortable closet, where sexual experimentation is admissible. Sexual diversity is, then, tolerated provided that it avoids scandal or public shame. The regime of what is visible and what can be named circumscribes sexualities. In fact, sexual dissidence is not unequivocally prohibited but controlled through the norms of secrecy and discretion. Someone who breaks these conventions is called *descarado* (literally, "faceless"), denoting shame and the loss of honor.

Knowing the queer

Rhetoric, body, law, and nation are implicated in Latin Americanist queer studies. The articulation of those categories creates a corpus in which exile, or the bodily experience of ostracization (that condition of not belonging to normative sexuality), is a point of departure to challenge the law, the ideal body promoted by the heteronormative state. Rhetorical configuration of literary works is the main focus of the essays included in the anthology *Reading and Writing the Ambiente: Queer Sexualities in Latino, Latin American, and Spanish Culture*, edited by Susana Chávez-Silverman and Librada Hernández (2000). In his introduction to this book, Robert R. Ellis (2000) declares that queer criticism emphasizes the "mechanisms through which sexuality can be discerned and known at all" (4). This statement suggests that a queer criticism addresses not only homosexuality but also much larger epistemological formulations, the representation and knowledge of sexuality, and its broad implications for the social edifice. While the anthologized criticism within this volume refers to specific literary works (Carmen Tisnado on Mario Benedetti, Robert M. Irwin on Xavier Villaurrutia, Emilio Bejel on Reinaldo Arenas, Librada Hernádez on Gómez de Avellaneda, and Rosemary G. Feal on Cortázar, among others) these essays are also always pieces of cultural reflection about bodies and social norms. These critics continually address the national construction of otherness, and specifically the politics of gender.

Queer studies are not only about self-representation of the queer subject but also about a circulation of queerness in the production, reception, prohibition, and disruption that occur within the patriarchal realm. *Reading and Writing the Ambiente* offers a view of a critical praxis addressing the epistemology of queerness. Departing from a close reading of rhetorical figurations that leads to an analysis of collective imaginaries within a postmodern and poststructuralist theoretical frame, these critiques expose contradictions, show fissures, and problematize hegemonic gender assumptions. Thus, rhetorical details such as an undefined subject, a gender ambiguity, a hyperbolic autobiography, or an ellipsis become the key elements to make visible a representational queerness. For queer studies, understanding rhetorical strategies is central to uncovering a politics involving the law and the representation of subjectivities. Queer critical discourse addresses the question of how queer subjectivity is both shaped by and shapes the law.

Let us look at a prominent example of this interaction between queer subjectivities and the state. The Chilean Nobel Prize winner Gabriela Mistral and the Argentinean intellectual Carlos Octavio Bunge were instrumental in modernizing the educational systems in Mexico and Argentina, but they both mostly kept their queerness hidden from the public—because, in both cases, the nations they were helping to build were defined as heterosexual, macho-centered, and culturally Catholic. To what extent should their writing and their public actions be interpreted as related to their queerness? The case of Bunge has been amply documented by Joseph M. Pierce (2013), who explores alternative forms of kinship and writing in the Bunge family, emphasizing the recomposition of gender roles and family dynamics as a kernel of modern transformation. For Pierce (2013), the Bunge family's queerness challenges traditional creole sex–gender principles, "questioning normative gender roles, complicating compulsory heterosexuality, and performing the gaps in the hegemonic division of public and private space" (2). The private recomposition of an order of kinship is not detached from what is produced in the public sphere. Latin Americanist queer scholarship quite often focuses on the queer cultural celebrity; by looking at such celebrities' public personae, their moral contradictions, and the excess of their characters, this body of work tries to make a queer intervention in the affairs of society at large. In fact, queer studies in Latin America consist of reading the canon to uncover what conventional criticism has concealed.

In her chapter "Alternative Identities of Gabriel(a) Mistral 1906–1920," Elizabeth Rosa Horan (2000) poses a queer view of Mistral's construction of subjectivity in her poetry. For this author, Mistral's poetic works have been misread and misappropriated by the official discourse, which mythologizes her as a "saint" and a "mother." In her reading, Horan underlines a queer aesthetics, pointing out the gender ambiguity of Mistral's poetic voice, the transgressing use of masculine values, and a unique painful sexuality. Language is a material that structures the enunciation of social norms. Horan's essay makes explicit that there is a hegemonic rhetoric that maintains the heteronormative edifying mandate. Edification is precisely the key word in the official propaganda of Mistral's persona. Nevertheless, what Horan (2000) also makes explicit is how, in her treatment of the rhetorical resources available in the poetic tradition, Mistral takes the position of outsiders, of foreigners "who, as voyeurs, aliens, look on the so-called normative human world" (170).

Based on literary and nonliterary sources, the book *A Queer Mother for the Nation: The State and Gabriela Mistral,* by Cuban American critic Licia Fiol-Matta (2002), displays images, attitudes, and ideological thoughts, not to construct an apology for the persona of Gabriela Mistral but to explore a deconstructionist interpretation of the discourses from and about this prominent figure of Latin American letters. Fiol-Matta's approach vacillates between mythologizing and dismantling Mistral's mythology, and her study suggests that the intervention of famous queer cultural icons in the formation of collective values is not insignificant. For Fiol-Matta, the persona of Gabriela Mistral is itself a fundamental part of the national iconography, and Mistral's social dimension is not just a public image designed according to the protocols and ideologies of public discourses. Rather, Fiol-Matta demonstrates that Mistral herself provided her own iconography. Gabriela Mistral, as an iconographic construction in the nation's imaginary, is a maternal figure whose queerness might be erased from the public narratives but is still unavoidable. Her queerness is a tacit one, a secret that is sustained by the close friends and family of the sexual dissident, so as to maintain the order of things, as Dominican anthropologist Carlos Ulises Decenas (2011) analyses in the configuration of the migrant Dominican gay identity (22).

The primary sources selected by Fiol-Matta (2002) are, for the most part, produced by others who have been in contact with Mistral, spectators witnessing her actions and appearances. Therefore, what Fiol-Matta is really reading is not the texts of Mistral but Mistral's reception—and not just the reception of Mistral's texts but of "Mistral" as an icon: Fiol-Matta investigates how a nonfeminine image can be readable as a body dedicated to the nation. Mistral as she is most often imagined—a woman without make-up—is a woman who has sacrificed the enjoyment of her own womanhood in favor of her public mission. Such a reading of Mistral's persona (essentially a hagiographic narrative) makes it possible to not deal with her "deviated" personality. In this slanted view of her biography, Mistral's queerness is replaced by the victimization of sexual violence: there occurs a sort of alchemy that sublimates any possibility of talking about Mistral's sexuality directly.

Still, we have to be careful. Any statement that pretends to explain Mistral's work and political activities based on the assumption she was a lesbian has to be nuanced by the fact that the identity of Gabriela Mistral is not shaped precisely by her sexuality but by homophobic discourse and closeting strategies. Nevertheless, Fiol-Matta (2002) makes us face a paradox: while on the one hand it is hard to find enough evidence to unequivocally show Mistral's homosexuality, on the other hand her image and attitudes have been read as constituting a queer presence. Homophobia and the performance of queerness are often woven together in the conception of the mother of the nation. The image of the traditional subjugated, weak, and dependable woman seems not to be enough to embody the titanic symbol of the emblematic mother. For that, it was necessary to propose a woman without those "feminine" inconveniences. Like in the case of the Bunge family in Argentina, queerness allows a configuration of the national by suspending homophobia and constructing a patriarchal mother, a phallic dominant figure, and a strong and solid image along the lines of the schoolteacher model. Thus, Gabriela Mistral is considered a figure, a gesture, and a performance serving the needs of the state. Reading those gestures, the surfaces of the icon, the design of the propaganda, and the aesthetics of maternity in the nation's education system, Fiol-Matta studies a phenomenon that has produced a total imaginary for the masses. With her performance, Mistral organizes the national symbolic space.

The Mexican minister of education José Vasconcelos invited the Chilean Gabriela Mistral to Mexico to help in the implementation of the Mexican cultural project. As Fiol-Matta's (2002) book explains, she was invited for the reason that Vasconcelos provided: "Es una rara" (She is a queer). It is a bit puzzling: if Mexican nationalism after the revolution was conceived of in heteronormative and patriarchal terms and with an explicitly homophobic agenda, why was Gabriela Mistral invited to participate in this enterprise? The answer is one based around practicality: it seems that revolutionary homophobia was not against queer performance as long as it was usable by the hegemonic interests. Thus, queerness is not necessarily a political dissidence but a strategic performance resulting from social rules, which are transgressed without being derogated. We have seen how feminizing the colonized is a strategy of domination, and the cross-dressing of political enemies is a form of disempowering them. The masculinization of Gabriela Mistral was the construction of a queer image not to dominate or disempower her but to amplify her civic value.

Dealing with the transgression of national figures—the symbolism that nourishes the imagination of communities— David Foster's (2000) essay "Evita Perón, Juan José Sebreli, and Gender" interrelates political discourses with idolatrous images and intellectual propositions. Evita Perón, the emblematic figure of Peronismo and the major figure of populism in Argentine history, has been appropriated by the Argentine gay movement. This appropriation queers the dominant discourse, which is one of the prevailing approaches in recent works of Latin American queer studies. The relationship between sexual dissidence and cultural and political hegemony has been studied in some of the most remarkable books of Latin American queer studies, such as Emilio Bejel's *Gay Cuban Nation* (2001), Fiol-Matta's *A Queer Mother for the Nation* (2002), James N. Green's *Beyond Carnival* (1999), and Ben Sifuentes-Jáuregui's *Transvestism, Masculinity, and Latin American Literature* (2002), where national identity is questioned from its own zone of denial.

To cover and to uncover:
From closet to scandal

The first chapter of Sifuentes-Jáuregui's *Transvestism, Masculinity, and Latin American Literature* (2002) is dedicated to the scandal of the aforementioned Ball of the 41, which in 1901 became a touchstone for Mexican homophobic speech of the beginning of the twentieth century. Sifuentes-Jáuregui addresses this topic with a reading spanning multiple texts and media: the novel by Ignacio E. Catrejón *Los cuarenta y uno* (The Forty-One) (1906); the caricature-like prints by José Guadalupe Posada that express both repudiation and fun; and newspaper articles. Across these representations of the scandal, Sifuentes-Jáuregui shows that homophobia and fascination with cross-dressing are two factors that materialize the emergence of queer politics in Latin America. Homophobia involves a panic toward the public display of the queer body.

Whereas Fiol-Matta (2002) follows the traces in the sublimated closeted texts to discover how queer images occupy a prominent position in the symbolic devices of the nation, Sifuentes-Jáuregui (2002) turns his attention to nonsublimated social texts, where the discourse surrounding the scandal attacks what was once private, violently making it a public issue. Both scholarly readings, however, concern how the national imaginary is constructed from parts of society that are wholly denied. These readings of society's most uncomfortable topics (either hidden or overexposed) discuss the rhetorical process of their reception instead of their enunciation. Fiol-Matta and Sifuentes-Jáuregui read readings, focusing on collective assumptions about strange bodies. These authors try to figure out how queer images are inserted into the collective.

Constructions of Latin American national identity are deeply related to the colonial unconscious; in light of this, Sifuentes-Jáuregui (2002) observes that Latin American national identity is continuously transvestized—in his own words, "the figuration of Latin American national identity and of transvestism are analogic" (10). Although this author states that transvestism in Latin America is considered a part of homosexual identity, his work goes beyond homoeroticism to focus on the heteronormative. This means that Sifuentes-Jáuregui's book points out how cross-dressing challenges heterosexual norms in addition to forming a transgender identity. By challenging the heteronormative gender-role system, transvestism carries out a radical political intervention that affects the whole gender system at large. The idea that gender is an external construction of performative gestures and not an essential biological determination may also be extrapolated to culture at large.

The reading-of-readings methodology in the works by Fiol-Matta and Sifuentes-Jáuregui consists of a deconstructive analysis aiming to uncover the mechanism of concealments and disclosures that makes possible a queer knowledge. According to Robert M. Irwin in his essay "As Visible as He Is: The Queer Enigma of Xavier Villaurrutia" (2000), it is the criticism of Villaurrutia's poetry, and not the poet himself, that has concealed homoeroticism in that poetry. "Appropriate" readings have traditionally preferred to maintain the enchantment of mystery, the semantic richness of ambiguity, rather than naming homoerotic desire—its subject, its object, its imaginary. Such a diffuse, aestheticist, or purist reading implies a homosexual panic on the part of critics more than a poetic closet in Villaurrutia's writing itself (Irwin 2000: 115). These remarks in Irwin's analysis are symptomatic of how queer readings operate; they break down critical prejudices about nonhegemonic desire by reading against the grain of literary criticism, and they capture the mechanisms that make alternative sexualities invisible.

Either by working within the darkness of the closet or by breaking the rules of visibility, the queer irruption itself can be accounted for as a manifestation of modernity (complying with Octavio Paz's (1987) definition of modernity as rupture). Queerness is an expression of rupture against compulsory heterosexuality and its method of excluding all types of difference. Nevertheless, this subtle queer intervention from the closeted intellectual may not be able to stake a claim to have asserted its influence within a larger social life and within institutions. Although reading the closet has produced much notable scholarship, and sexuality is at present a prominent field of knowledge, that political incidence of queerness can be understood as implicit, disguised, and constrained to close and exclusive spaces. The rupture that, according to Paz (1987), characterizes modern tradition has its effect in the aesthetic practice of the lettered city (17). This is not to discount the importance of public scandals within the stage of modern politics; however, these irruptions of scandal should not be read simply as political action alone because they are very parts of the performance of daily life and by their very nature constitute a challenge to gender norms.

Alternative sexuality played the game of secrecy, but it did not hide enough or, better said, it became a rhetorical and political challenge to make visible what was shut away from view. Even with their (not-very-well) hidden sexual dissidence and their ambiguous public personae, queer intellectuals became the center of attention. Colombian literary critic Jaime Manrique (1999) points out this paradox of being marginal and influential at the same time. Four biographical essays comprise his book *Eminent Maricones: Arenas, Lorca, Puig, and Me.* With a very personal view, Manrique details the life experience and the textual production of Reinaldo Arenas, Federico García Lorca, Manuel Puig, and Manrique himself. His narration, filtered through his distinctive ethnographic and sociological gaze, creates a unique texture for his prose that depicts the complexity of nomadic subjects who are renowned for the literary audience. These authors share the condition of being in exile due to their dissident intellectual position and their sexuality. Furthermore, they challenge the moral systems of intolerant societies in the Hispanic world. Nevertheless, challenging morality and being in exile—physically as well as intellectually—makes them prominent. Manrique displays his gallery of heroes as a sort of hagiography, depicting the private life of writers who produced images, symbols, and subjectivities that, being unconventional, are valuable aesthetically. This valorization of queerness within the domain of literary production supports the notion that rhetoric is one of the main criteria for determining prestige and social worth for those with alternative sexualities.

The Mexican intellectual Salvador Novo and the Colombian poet and journalist Porfirio Barba Jacob are two instances of public figures who did not stay hidden behind the walls of discretion like most public queer figures did. Instead, they brought their critical lenses to bear on the public stage without hiding their queerness from public curiosity. In contrast to most queer public intellectuals, their very persona is constructed as a challenge to the sex–gender order, opening the door not only to their own intimacy but also to the underground practices that cultural scruples have largely relegated to the realm of the obscene. Both poets dare to name their homoerotic desire without decorum; their writing is highly autobiographical and confessional to the point of being frightful for those who were in danger of being alluded to in their chronicles. Scandal itself articulates a form of queer politics when it confronts norms of discretion and the constraints of the closet. In fact, the exceptional examples of Novo and Barba Jacob prove that modern strategies to place homosexuality outside of society's definitions of the "normal" are not effective. Although Novo was repeatedly involved in scandals, his intellectual influence and his work did not occupy a marginal place in Mexican letters. Creativity and an extravagant lifestyle of recreation (often characterized by alcohol, drugs, and sex excess) have been linked in the construction of the modern artist since Romanticism; Barba Jacob fulfills this ideal portrait of the artist while being one of the main figures of modern queer transgression. The public personae and creativity of both Novo and Barba Jacob show the way that modernity legitimates queerness. These authors' method of "coming out" is not equivalent to the one prescribed for gay politics after the Stonewall riots in Manhattan in 1969. Their insolence toward the society of secrets was a political gesture of breaking the barriers of shame. They aimed neither to organize a liberation movement nor to prescribe a certain cultural practice: their openness was a rebellious expression articulated as an artistic disruption closer to the idea of *épater le bourgeois* of the avant-gardes' decadent experimentation than to civil rights militancy. In that sense, their coming out was an aesthetic project, provided by the tradition of the rupture of modernity. Their queerness was finally a confirmation of modern ideology. In the study of Latin American public figures, queer scholars have challenged modern and nationalistic homophobia through assigning aesthetic value to queerness. From decorum to scandal, heteronormative national discourses are constantly called into question by queer visibility at the center of cultural debates, as we will see in the following section.

Queer resistance

In 1925 and 1932, Mexico City's newspapers published a series of articles about the controversy surrounding revolutionary culture, virility, and effeminacy. Daniel Balderston (1998), Víctor Díaz Arciniega (1989), Mary Kendall Long (1995), Carlos Monsiváis (1998), and Guillermo Sheridan (1985, 1999), among others, have studied this controversy as one of those moments in public debate that make visible the contradictions between modernity, sexuality, and nationality. The preoccupation of attributing to the nation a heterosexual character authorizes an intense scorn of homoerotic practices. In the newspaper articles about the controversy, homosexuality is depicted alternately as social decadence, a highly contagious disease, or a weakening of virility that threatens the nation's revolutionary institutions. It is a state priority to prevent the malady of effeminacy in literature and public life. In February 1925, an article asserted that "bureaucracy kills virility in intellectuals; that's why eunuchs abound in offices ... literature becomes smaller and effeminate" (quoted in Díaz Arciniegas 1989: 115, my translation). In this way, effeminacy is associated with a lack of nationalism, an absence of social engagement, and a lack of historical consciousness (an essential factor in the construction of national identity). According to these homophobic journalists, the state's public figures (intellectuals, artists, bureaucrats, etc.) had established a set of mannerisms that conveyed a false comprehension (i.e., their effeminacy produced gender confusion); they were deceptive and, deep down, did not appropriately represent Mexican nationalism. The official revolutionary state incorporated this homophobic critique and demanded a virile literature, as the minister of public education, José Manuel Puig Casauranc stated in his inaugural discourse: he said that his administration would "not promote Mexican artworks with mannerisms and gender indefinition"; instead, his office would "support those projects that reflect life as it is: severe and sometimes cold" (quoted in Díaz Arciniegas 1989: 89, my translation). The nation was then defined by a gendered aesthetics: it must be tough, realist, and virile. The state established a policy that would serve as the point of reference to which all sexual diversity was compared. This new credo established a zone of abjection and allowed the state to point out the enemies of the nation and to correct them through scorn. Through these new policies, the state could effectively dispose of bodies deemed ill (the undesirable other) in order to keep the privileges of the national, heterosexual, and macho self. For almost the entire twentieth century, a complex cultural apparatus was established that made use of all the forms of high culture (or the lettered city) and popular culture as well as law enforcement: this coordinated institutional system allowed the state to keep those antinational queer subjects out of citizenship.

However, it was in the lettered city, expressed in the newspapers and other public venues, where the first gestures of queer resistance took place. The group of artists and writers gathered around the literary magazine *Contemporáneos*, which promoted a cosmopolitan form of avant-garde and published texts in which homosexual desire was unequivocally represented, defied the homophobic public policy of the revolutionary state. Many of the members of this group were under attack. The former minister of education José Vasconcelos had appointed some of them in posts related to arts and cultural promotion. An open letter published in 1934 by a group of self-proclaimed revolutionary artists asked for the resignation of these appointees of Vasconcelos, who were accused of not being able to represent a revolutionary ideology and the nation interests due to their "doubtful psychological condition" (quoted in Balderston 1998: 62, my translation). As in the case of the Cuban debate regarding Spanish male prostitutes, the medicalization of queerness was an instrument of national sanitation, deeming homoeroticism an illness that would corrupt the nation-state project.

It is not correct to say that this exposition of the *Contemporáneos* group succeeded in expelling queerness and gender issues from public conversations. It is arguable that one of the main consequences of this controversy was the criticism of the model of maleness promoted by the state, the macho, which from the 1930s became one of the most prevalent topics among Mexican intellectuals. Prominent figures such as Rosario Castellanos, Carlos Fuentes, Octavio Paz, and Samuel Ramos, to name a few of the most visible, developed a criticism of the macho figure as one of the main obstacles to modernization, whose deconstruction, along with the aestheticization of homoeroticism in the works by the *Contemporáneos* group, can be counted as the foundational works on queer issues in Mexico. In one of the most canonical essays in Mexican literature, *El laberinto de la soledad* (The Labyrinth of Solitude) (1950), by the Nobel Prize-winning Octavio Paz, we can read that homoeroticism and machismo are not opposed, showing that homoeroticism is, in fact, one of the main components of the characterization of macho. The macho subject is a sum of ambiguities: he is hermetic and explosive, fearful and terrifying, simulator and unconfident, violent and submissive. These contradictions can be taken as queer aspects of the colonized masculinity. We cannot understand Latin American queerness without referring to the colonial root of maleness. It constitutes a forceful deviation from the Western norm (and to be clear the Western norm at issue here is the Spaniard version of the main cultural basis of masculinity—i.e., the *vir* of the conqueror, the unattainable model of man that structures macho anxiety). Octavio Paz's (2004) analysis of the oral Mexican tradition of the *albur* (Mexico's famous conversational battles, consisting of exchanging double entendres charged with symbols of violent eroticism) shows that the homosocial male relationship is defined by a constant impulse of *chingar* (etymologically, "to rape") the other in order to subdue him, at least symbolically. The macho is defined by its capacity for domination of other men; the prestige of virility is assigned to the one who exercises violence in this verbal homoerotic rape (Paz 2004: 84–85).

Conclusion

As in the deconstructing effect of transvestism on the gender structure on which the nation is funded, read in Sifuentes-Jáuregui's (2002) study of cross-dressing, the queering of the macho that we find in Mexican intellectuals' essays shows that the intervention of queer politics is materialized in the effect of finding queerness inside hegemonic discourses and practices. While queerness is conceived of as a zone of exclusion, the negative projection of the nation, its very rejection, is the first step for its political constitution. In the upper classes and the intellectual elite, the space for a queer culture is formed under the rules of discretion, to which scandal is its constitutive exception. Queerness infiltrates literature, the arts, and public debates to the point that the nation (while nominally constructed according to heterosexual norms) has to admit queerness as part of its narrative. This does not mean that queerness is a specific form of ideology that was propagated inside dominant groups in a conspiratorial way; rather, queerness is an intrinsic resistance to the intent of any ruling sexuality or gender expression. The queer irruption in culture should then be understood as a responsive position—a necessary rebellion against bodily constraints—in an intimate event or in social practice.

The impact of Latin American queer studies goes beyond the domain of sexuality itself, raising fundamental questions about national identities and the crisis of identities in general. Critical works such as the ones reviewed in these pages are less defining than questioning. According to this body of work, no gender or sex category that implies the natural, the essential, and the normal can be legitimized after being reduced to artificial gestures, and that is when queer analysis comes to challenge the patriarchal system. This challenge implies not only a review of moral and aesthetic thoughts but also the destabilization of the social and/or symbolic system at large. The project of queering the nation looks for traces of concealed desires and finds there a rich source of rhetorical inventions that can be used in an aesthetic strategy to introduce what is deemed abject in the very cultural production of the lettered city. This undercover strategy of introducing queerness in the public discourse is not the only one queer authors have utilized to queer the modern system of significations and the politics of exclusion. Cross-dressing and the challenges that scandal poses to the heteronormative hegemony have opened the way to introducing a deep critique of the entire gender system and the political relations it determines. Modernity is then a period of Latin American history in which queerness has had a prominent role in transforming social life to the point that it is possible to assert that modernization can also be viewed as a process of queering itself.

CHAPTER 3

LGBT politics and culture

In Latin America, the gay and lesbian liberation movement appeared in the context of the Cold War, which means the discourses, organizational features, and political strategies of the movement were related to the broader political struggle that characterized the Latin American public sphere from the 1960s to the 1980s. My argument is that the Latin American gay and lesbian movement, despite its clear relation to the LGBT movement in the United States, is not necessarily a continuation of North American diversity politics and is better described in terms of the logic of political and cultural constraints that defined the Latin American symbolic landscape of the time.[1] The Frente de Liberación Homosexual (Front of Homosexual Liberation) in Argentina, founded in 1967, and the Frente de Liberación Homosexual in Mexico, founded in 1971, initiated their political activities in the middle of the Manichean tensions of the Cold War. In both cases, the discourse included Marxist revolutionary language combined with

[1] It should be noted, however, that a socialist agenda was present and influential in the US LGBT movement at various points, as works by Susan Stryker (2008) and Sherry Wolf (2009) show.

feminist principles, as well as concrete demands regarding abuse of power and social homophobia. All of these discourses served to inscribe their agenda into the logic of liberationist struggles. But, in its development, the Latin American gay and lesbian movement experienced an uneasy relationship with Marxist-inspired parties and organizations, even though LGBT organizations consistently maintained leftist positions. Given that tension, the queering effect of the gay and lesbian movement in Latin America occupies an in-between space of intervention in the public sphere. It is this unstable queering intervention in the spaces of Latin American civil society that will be the main focus of this chapter.

We cannot, however, assert that it was in the 1970s that politics advocating sexual diversity first appeared in the region's history. It is important to recall that positioning against homophobia had already been implicit in the fin-de-siècle aesthetics of *modernismo*, and it had been an explicit subject of public debates since the 1920s in postrevolutionary Mexico, as discussed in Chapter 2. The lettered city saw the establishment of the basis of the crisis of heteronormative and macho culture, by applying seductive and disruptive rhetorical strategies that visualized sex–gender differences and deconstructed patriarchal assumptions and biases. In any case, since the 1960s, the homosexual liberation organizations have gone beyond the avant-garde illustrious elite, following and inscribing themselves into the resistance culture of the left. Although they seem to be contrasting, the modern lettered city of the first decade of the twentieth century and the 1970s liberation groups had in common a contradictory relationship with revolutionary ideologies. Both became agents of queering revolutionary politics by intending to instill sexual liberation demands within revolutionary proposals.

The history of antihomophobic resistance in Mexico can be traced back to the group of artists and writers gathered around the magazine *Contemporáneos* in the 1920s and 1930s, and specifically to certain poetry by Salvador Novo and Xavier Villaurrutia and artworks by Abraham Ángel, Augustin Lazo, Roberto Montenegro, and Manuel Rodríguez Lozano. Attentive to the homophilic—that is to say, nonhomophobic—works produced in Europe during that era, these first attempts at dignifying the image of homosexuality and alternative lifestyles inform us about the process that the politics of gender would develop into in Mexico later in the century. Given that these homophilic ideas were imported from imperialist nations (these authors translated works by French homosexual writers such as André Gide), these works also carried the burden of being labeled as colonialist and reactionary, and as threats to national identity. Europeanizing suspicions also appear with respect to some of the writers grouped around the Cuban literary magazine *Origenes* (1944–1956), which also maintained a homophilic position. But those pre-gay-movement attempts were articulated in the context of intellectual disputes and did not permeate the discourses of political parties; that is, they did not yet constitute a politics capable of influencing state institutions.

The libertarian age

In his comparative study of the gay movements in Mexico and Brazil, Rafael de la Dehesa (2010) asserts gay political positioning started to be articulated in the 1960s in tandem with the increasing use of human rights discourse to connote modernization, as had the women's suffrage movement in the late nineteenth century (3). If human rights is the discursive matrix that tends to open the gate to a homosexual's citizenship, then we can argue that gay and lesbian movements in Latin America construct the homosexual subject on the basis of the defense of a victim considered unequal from the position of heterodominant discourse. This claim refers back to the heterosexual–homosexual crisis that characterized modernity, which Eve Kosowsky Sedgwick discusses in her *Epistemology of the Closet* (1990: 1). The universalizing heterosexual assumption is disavowed when the gender order's exclusionary nature and its hegemony come to be questioned alongside the mere existence of homosexual identities. Negotiating a space in the political sphere and making possible changes in constitutional frames in order to include sexual diversity within the scope of citizenry has been a process that, according to de la Dehesa (2010), depends on the strategic use of the international accords on human rights related to sex and gender (4).

The first recognized gay and lesbian political organization would emerge in Argentina in 1967, two years before the Stonewall riots, which marked the beginning of the US LGBT movement. After Héctor Anabitarte was expelled from the Communist Party because of his homosexuality, he and a group of Marxist queer middle-class intellectuals formed the group Nuestro Mundo (Our World) in Buenos Aires with the goal to stop heterosexist repression, which was being expressed in the form of police detentions and extortions (Díez 2015: 76). In 1971, Nuestro Mundo became the Frente de Liberación Homosexual (FLH) (Bilbao 2012: 24). Bárbara Soledad Bilbao (2012) notes that leftist political parties deemed the FLH to be a proponent of a sectarian form of politics and useless to the revolutionary cause. In fact, the FLH always complained about feeling marginalized from left-wing organizations. Nonetheless, the FLH claimed to be anti-imperialist, anticapitalist, and liberationist, emphasizing that the oppression of women and men by men (i.e., the uneven nature of the gender structure) was at the root of the system of oppression (quoted in Bilbao 2012: 30). By focusing on the gendered root of oppression, the FLH showed its proposal was a radical plan for resignifying the revolutionary agenda by introducing the patriarchal dimension of the oppressive system as the target of revolutionary ideology, in line with Marxist and feminist positions. In the document "Sexo y Revolución" (Sex and Revolution), a manifest of the FLH published in 1973, the private, day-to-day politics of the body was presented as the kernel of domination. The family is, then, an institution that reproduces individuals who will be useful in the capitalist system of exploitation. Thus, a real revolutionary act would consist of dismantling the oppressive structure of the family. The heterosexual order, under the dominion of machismo, would be defeated in order to achieve real liberation. For the FLH, homoeroticism is thus dangerous for the macho order, as it disavows the very order of domination. "Sex and Revolution" saw in the liberation of sexual practices from heterosexual/patriarchal constraints the main factor in the struggle against capitalism (Frente de Liberación Homosexual 2011).

This criticism of the family as an organizational basis of oppression was also one of the main arguments that Mexican activists for sexual diversity brought to the leftist organizations in the 1970s. According to LGBT Mexican activist Alejandro Brito, this criticism of the family as a conservative and harmful institution was enhanced with the influence of the general sexual liberation and the feminist movements (quoted in Estrada Corona 2010). The social movements of the 1960s and 1970s in Mexico were focused on correcting the authoritarianism of the Mexican revolution following Marxist criteria as the path to democratization. This blended context influenced the gay rights movement, as what is considered the first public gay demonstration actually consisted of a handful of protesters within the march on October 2, 1978, commemorating the tenth anniversary of the massacre of students in Tlatelolco by the Mexican army. It is important to remember, nevertheless, that according to José María Covarrubias (one of the most renowned LGBT activists in Mexico), in 1972, the Frente de Liberación Homosexual Mexicana (Mexican Homosexual Liberation Front) held a march protesting the Vietnam War, a fact that would support the idea that the Mexican gay liberation movement synchronized with similar protests carried out by the movement's North American counterparts (cited in Mogrovejo 2000: 64).

Rather than the predominant antiauthoritarian profile of the civil rights politics that engendered the North American gay movement, Mexican gay activism was more embedded in the socialist agenda, which helped to determine most of its political inefficacy.[2] Similar to what happened with leftist socialist and communist parties, the gay and lesbian activist groups in the 1970s (Movimiento de Liberación Homosexual de México (Mexican Homosexual Liberation Movement), Sex-Pol, Lesbos, and others) tended to fall apart because of disagreements over ideological positions, dogmatism, and differences of opinion over organizational issues (Hernández Cabrera 2005: 290). The same criticism that José Revueltas expresses in his essays and novels with respect to the disorganization and dogmatism of the Mexican Communist Party could be applied to the errors that dismantled the first lesbian–gay organizations in Mexico. In this sense, the Mexican LGBT movement is inscribed in the panorama of practices and vices of the Latin American left during the 1970s. Porfiro M. Hernández Cabrera (2005) lists the factors that contributed to the crisis of the Movimiento de Liberación Homosexual de México, themselves very similar to those José Revueltas (1978) has pointed out with respect to leftist political practices:

> Internal struggles for power; disconnectedness from the base; the pretension by Mexico City groups that they were national representatives; the inefficient organization following partisan models; the *machismo* of some lesbians; the tearful denunciations of persecution; the absence of an attractive sexual-political agenda which would generate cohesion; the lack of artistic and intellectual support which became a lack of "theoretical support." (291)

---

[2] Other radical agendas were present, although with lesser impact, in the US LGBT movement. The support of Black Panthers and the pairing of LGBT groups with the Chicago workers' movement and protests against the Vietnam War in the 1970s are instances of this interaction.

This makes clear how the dependence of the Mexican LGBT movement on the communist model worked to reproduce organizational vices.

A sort of Marxist–Leninist organizational morality impinged upon the actions, slogans, and style of the movement around the continent. But only in some of the leftist organizations was LGBT politics really supported, as in the case of the Partido Revolucionario de los Trabajadores (Workers' Revolutionary Party) in Mexico in the 1980s and Convergência Socialista (Socialist Convergence) in Brazil (de la Dehesa 2010: 62). The contemporary left parties in Argentina, Mexico, and Uruguay would be more inclined to support LGBT proposals than those of the 1970s, as Jordi Díez (2015) explains in his comparative analysis of the advancement of same-sex rights in Argentina, Chile, and Mexico. For Díez (2015), the penetration of LGBT activists in the government through their alliance with central-left and liberal parties was definitive for achieving the legal recognition of gay marriage in Argentina and Mexico (8–9).

Nevertheless, many of the socialist leaders in Latin America did not welcome sexual diversity as a revolutionary identity. The persecution of homosexuals in Cuba in the late 1960s and 1970s is paradigmatic of this rejection. In that case, as in the Mexican revolution in the 1920s and 1930s, nonheterosexual expressions were read as bourgeois decadence, antinational, and counterrevolutionary. Events such as the expulsion of the poet Allen Ginsberg, who sympathized with the revolution and was deported after telling a joke declaring his willingness to sleep with the *comandantes*, were added to a general disappointment with revolution among a host of global intellectuals that had been triggered by writer Reinaldo Arenas' and poet Heberto Padilla's censorship and persecution (Quiroga 2000: 125).[3] While

---

[3] Besides the Beat Generation group, we can mention intellectuals such as Octavio Paz, José Revueltas, Jean-Paul Sartre, and Mario Vargas Llosa, among many others.

homophilic representation of sexual dissidence was part of the repertoire of prerevolutionary literature in Cuba, the revolutionary regime deemed that publishing or exhibiting these works would be dangerous to the new state. In Cuba, being homosexual was a criterion for being denied citizenship, with other excluded groups including religious leaders and intellectuals who criticized Castro's regime.

I want to underline the contrast between the Argentinean FLH's sexualized theorization of the revolution in its manifesto "Sex and Revolution" and the Cuban homophobic socialism; these were the two poles between which the politics of sexual diversity fluctuated. While in Argentina and Mexico a queer resignification of revolution anchored LGBT activism to the leftist utopia, mainstream socialism in Cuba forced sexual diversity into a position against revolutionary ideology. The Cuban writer Reinaldo Arenas is the main example of homosexual resistance to Castro's totalitarian socialism. Arenas was condemned for abusing two boys, even though they retracted the accusation. He was a dissident writer, so the story of the boys can be taken as an excuse for repressing him. He was forced to publically incriminate himself and to desist from his criticism of the government. According to Emilio Bejel (2001), Arenas' writing project was to oppose the coercive power of the state, which did not allow him to be a gay man and to create (146).

José Quiroga (2000) notes that the new left in the United States and Europe, as well as in many sectors of the left in Argentina, Brazil, and Mexico, includes the LGBT agenda under the feminist principle that the personal is political; in contrast, in Cuba, the persecution of homosexuals is institutionalized (129). The UMAP (the Spanish acronym for Military Units of Production Assistance), established in 1965, were centers of incarceration and forced work intended to correct antisocial individuals deemed to be obstacles to the process of the creation of the new man—the utopian proposal of Ernesto "Che" Guevara for the citizenship resulting from the revolution. For the official discourse, homosexuality, like religion, prostitution, and addictions, were vices inherited from the previous republican regime, and individuals affected by them should be re-educated through work and discipline and be indoctrinated with the socialist ideology (Sierra Madero 2006: 197). In the 1970s, the homophobic nature of the revolution was expressed in the rules excluding the LGBT population from a number of jobs, rights to housing, and prohibition on participation in the Communist Party. In an interview with the Mexican journalist Carmen Lira Saade (2010), Fidel Castro recognized that persecuting homosexuals was a big mistake that had motivated the international dissatisfaction with the Cuban revolution. Old prejudices, not old vices, were the obstacles for the revolutionary project. A similar traditional patriarchal view still nurtures the discourse of leftist leaders in the twenty-first century: the homophobic declarations of the presidents Hugo Chávez (Venezuela), Rafael Correa (Ecuador), Nicolás Maduro (Venezuela), and Evo Morales (Bolivia) are widely known instances of this patriarchal leftist view.[4]

In July 2015, I was fortunate to meet Milú Vargas, a pro-human-rights politician and important advocate for women and sexual diversity in Nicaragua. I was interested in knowing her view on the status of women and issues of sexual diversity in the revolutionary regime in that country. In 1987, Vargas and Rita Arauz were responsible for including lesbianism in the Encuentro Latinoamericano sobre Mujeres y Legislación (Latin American Summit on Women and Legislation). After an attempt on the part of the leaders of the Frente Sandinista de Liberación Nacional

---

[4] In their introduction to the volume *Queering Paradigms V* (2016), Manuela Lavinas Picq and María Amelia Viteri note an ambiguity toward sexual diversity by Ecuadorian president Rafael Correa: while he shows support to transgender activist Diane Rodríguez, he expresses statements against same-sex marriage (1–2). Homophobic statements by Nicolás Maduro and Evo Morales have received criticism from those politicians' leftist LGBT supporters (Aznares 2013; Molina 2015).

(Sandinista Front of National Liberation, FSLN) to reprimand the organizers for including this topic, the committee argued that the FSLN should neither oppose nor promote topics relating to sexual diversity. I would like to highlight those arguments, as they reveal the political conjunctures where a LGBT politics emerges: a) gender and sexual issues are relevant in human rights politics and any legislative conversation cannot ignore them; b) international solidarity has been a key element in the legitimation and defense of the Nicaraguan Revolution, and so, as a large proportion of the supporters of the revolution are LGBT, it is not coherent politics to repress LGBT people; c) the Cuban precedents (such as the case of Reinaldo Arenas) would encourage the suspicion that the Nicaraguan Revolution is a dictatorship; and d) opposing LGBT rights would make supporters of the FSLN seem less modern and therefore conservative. But, still, these arguments were not enough to advance any LGBT agenda in Nicaragua. It is telling that consensual homosexual relations were banned until 2007 (Morel 2007).

The tension between the revolutionary left and the politics of homosexuality is a constant locus in the narratives of literature and cinema. Works such as *El beso de la mujer araña* (The Kiss of the Spider Woman) (1976) by Manuel Puig, a prominent Argentinean writer who was member of the FLH; *El lobo, el bosque y el hombre nuevo* (The Wood, the Wolf and the New Man) (1990) by the Cuban Senel Paz; and *Tengo miedo, torero* (I'm Afraid, Bullfighter) (2001) by the Chilean Pedro Lemebel deploy intense dialogues in which the trend is to conciliate leftist politicians with the homosexual. Both subjectivities converge in the condition of oppression. In the case of *El beso de la mujer araña*, the oppression of the working-class leader is translated into the terms of the condemnation of sexual dissidence; in *El bosque el lobo y el hombre nuevo*, revolutionary discourse comes to value the contributions of gays to national culture, arguing for their citizenship; and in *Tengo miedo, torero* the political goal of defeating Augusto Pinochet's dictatorship is contextualized within a homoerotic romance, replacing the classic heteronormative national romance narratives that are the dominant discourse in Latin America, according to literary critic Doris Sommer (1991).

In his manifesto "Hablo por mi diferencia" (I Speak for My Difference), Pedro Lemebel (2000) points out the double oppression of queers at the economic periphery of society, positioning sexual diversity (in the 1980s, when the manifesto was released, the most marginal of the revolutionary sectors) as the most dissident extreme. This poem-manifesto was read for the first time at a public event of the Socialist Party (Partido Socialista Chileno) in 1986. The addressees, the socialist comrades, are the point of reference to establish a difference in the level of oppression of the working class versus people who are poor and queer:

Yo no voy a cambiar por el marxismo
Que me rechazó tantas veces
No necesito cambiar
Soy más subversivo que usted

(I'm not going to change because of Marxism
Which rejected me many times
I don't need to change
I'm more subversive than you). (Lemebel 2000: 96)

Lemebel's activism focused on the margin of the margins, as he declared in an interview with Pedro Carcuro on the program *De pe a pa* (From Here to There) on Chilean national television in November 2000. In that extreme marginality, alternative identity depends on the reception of homophobic insults. This confrontation of the leftist machismo brings the marginal body into the political sphere, which is one of the most relevant effects of queering leftist politics. From the manifesto "Sex and Revolution" by the Argentine FLH to the poem "Hablo por mi deferencia" by Pedro Lemebel, the proposal of queering the resistant forces of society located the object of revolutionary liberation not in institutional reorganization but in cultural reorganization: that very intimate zone of culture we call the body. Gay politics demands the right to be respected for being different.

Gay culture in Latin America

In a text commemorating the fifteenth anniversary of Gay–Lesbian Culture Week (June 2001), an event that since 1987 has gathered the most important LGBT artistic and intellectual expressions in Mexico, Carlos Monsiváis (2001) offers a lexical distinction that seems useful for understanding the transformation that Mexican sexual culture has experienced since the introduction of the concept of gayness along with gay politics and lifestyle:

> gay is not a synonym of "*homosexual, maricón, puto, tortillera, invertido, sodomita,*" but rather a word which names attitudes, organizations, and behaviors that were unknown until recently. In the same way coming out of the closet used to be an action tied to shamelessness and the cynicism of those who had nothing to lose, but is now an act which proclaims the legitimacy of difference. (9)

"Gayness" marks a watershed in Mexican sexual culture. It is a concept that is not synonymous with *tortillera, maricón, puto,* or *invertido,* although it refers to very similar practices.[5] The semantic

---

[5] *Tortillera* is a slang term, often pejorative, used in Mexico to refer to lesbians. *Maricón, puto,* and *invertido,* also pejorative, refer to homosexual males: *maricón* connotes effeminacy, *invertido* conveys dissidence from heterosexuality, and the meaning of *puto* is associated with clandestine sexuality.

precision proposed by Monsiváis focuses on how those words used for slander in Mexican traditional homophobia came to be replaced by the vindicating word "gay," a concept tied to happiness, pride, community, and the declaration of the legitimacy of difference. From this angle, the introduction of the word "gay" to the Latin American lexicon underlined the creation of a space of liberation and the designation of a legitimate social identity. To wit, this was the creation of a culture that would embrace subjects previously scorned because of their sexual preference. The LGBT movement then aimed to pursue liberation from homophobia. However, the terms of that liberation were unclear. To liberate implies an abolition of exclusion. But, in the LGBT case, the notion of liberation echoed the principles of the sexual liberation movement, in which the body is the core of politics and the body is freed from the various forms of control. The right of women to decide over their reproductive functions, the right to love regardless of sexual orientation, and the right to sex free from institutional surveillance are the main lines of the general sex liberation agenda. In this context, liberation from homophobia established a utopian ultimate goal, which represented a further level of liberation than the one offered by socialist ideology. This gay revolutionary thought would henceforth be highlighted every time homophobic expressions were made public. Like the sexual liberation movement, the LGBT movement was first defined in revolutionary terms, under the political rhetoric of the left, as discussed above. But its location of the revolutionary was no longer the working class. The concrete site of struggle was moral. The prevalence of religious biases in the state laws and procedures called for a more legal and cultural field of action.

Even though there were contradictions in the conceptions of revolution of LGBT politics and of the majoritarian left, solidaristic connections with common causes established strong links between militants in the various resistance movements. In the 1990s in Argentina, Chile, and Mexico, antidiscrimination reforms relating to sexual diversity were made possible thanks to the links between LGBT leaders and leftist allies. Finally, the notion of recognizing disenfranchised people was common to leftist liberation politics and human rights proponents (Díez 2015: 198–199). Rafael de la Dehesa (2010) asserts that one of the central changes in the LGBT movements of Mexico and Brazil in the 1980s "was a paradigm shift from homosexual liberation to homosexual rights" (5). This meant a divorce from universalist revolutionary conceptions, whose utopian generalization of human beings reduced sexual diversity to heterosexuality. It also meant a divorce between the sexual revolution and the favoring of ideas of equal rights, including the right to marriage, representing a departure from the sexual revolution's former anti-family militancy. These facts show not only that LGBT politics distanced itself from traditional leftist positions but also that the new left, which had access to parliamentary power, redirected its discourse to so-called minority rights by supporting LGBT and feminist agendas.

The appearance of gayness on the Latin American cultural horizon was part of a larger history of influences and translations of North American and European cultural and political processes and as such was marked by a mixture of acceptance and resistance, as was the case with many of the ideas and fashions emanating from the United States. As Jordi Díez (2015) points out, it is because of international pressures linked to trade agreements that countries such as Chile and Mexico have implemented anti-discrimination reforms (198). But the gay rights movement faces the greatest obstacles to being admitted into many Latin American societies, mainly because homosexuality is considered a threat to national identity or public morality, or, as in the cases of the Cuban and Mexican revolutions, is seen as reactionary, colonialist, and procapitalist. Traditionally, the homosexual has been an *other* whose exclusion defines national identity, as seen in Chapter 2. Gay culture thus would be part of the process of North-

Americanization that has threatened nationality. This contradiction is essential to understanding gay politics before homophobia: gayness liberated sexual dissidents from nationalistic homophobic culture, which had been especially scathing because of the need to define national profiles through exclusion. In this context, national foundations were built upon slander, which now implies that the consolidation of gay culture will dismantle the bases of homophobia and gendered nationalistic discourses. Gender connotations are central to collective cultural definitions in the majority of popular music genres that represent nationalistic concepts: *ranchera* films and *corridos* in Mexico, tango in Argentina, *llaneras* in Venezuela, *boleros* in the Caribbean, *saudades* in Brazil, and *valsecitos criollos* in Peru. In these genres, the virile figure is privileged as the national model of the male gender, and gayness had to find a way to be inserted into the nationalistic framework or accept the stigma of the outsider and marginalized other.

The confrontation of national homophobia with a gay rights agenda marked a profound shift in the political coordinates in which nationalistic politics now had to give way to those of civil rights. This must in fact necessarily be seen as an effect of globalizing politics, as various authors have suggested (e.g., Altman 2001; Cruz-Malavé and Manalansan 2002; Hawley 2001). Given this globalizing and suspiciously colonizing intervention, some leftist leaders in Latin America have been clearly homophobic in their public statements and policies, as aforementioned. The complex collapsing of political discourses and conflicting meanings makes sexual diversity a very controversial topic in the present politics of Latin America. Sexuality seems to be one of the most unresolved human rights issues in the region. The adaptations and resignification of the Latin American LGBT movement had to respect global trends, inscribing this activism within the processes of the appropriation and redirection of metropolitan models.

In an unpublished 2001 interview I conducted with the Chilean writer and activist Juan Pablo Sutherland, he pointed out that a certain critical position defines this redirection of gayness in the language of decolonization: for Sutherland, the explosion of gay culture in Chile came with the implementation of neoliberal policies in the early 1990s. A model of frivolous, consumerist gay culture came to impose an aesthetic that domesticated the gay population, making its members useful to the capitalist system. Sutherland suggests that gay identity includes a socioeconomic factor in its characterization. Is then LGBT politics a middle-class, urban politics? The quotation from Carlos Monsiváis at the start of this section states that gay is not a synonym of *maricón*, *puto*, *tortillera*, or any other Mexican derogatory term for nonheterosexual individuals, and this is because those identities are out of the middle-class comfort zone, in the unsafe field of popular homophobia. Pedro Lemebel, on his part, declared in the aforementioned interview for Chilean national television that his work was focused on those sectors identified with homophobic terms, those people who were known through the language of hate. These intellectuals suggest there is a class intersection we need to take into account in order to situate queer politics in Latin America, remembering that not all diverse sexual practices are embraced by the acronym LGBT. Beyond the marketing glamour there is a field of sexual expressions and gender transgressions that exist outside gay politics and culture. Gay intellectuals such as Lemebel and Sutherland have opened a critical space where the notion of the liberation of middle-class, urban gay politics has to consider a social space dominated by sex–gender violence, where the life and death of sexual diversity is determined by homophobic rules.

The use of the term "gay" denotes a homosexual who belongs to the middle class, is educated, travels, and lives in the city. To live as a gay, then, contrasts with living as a *joto*, *chichifo*, or *mayate* (for example), all of whom belong to a culture of oppression in which effeminate men are the most frequent targets of homophobic violence.[6] Guillermo Núñez Noriega observes that the term "gay" in Mexico is used as a euphemism for *joto*, which undermines the original political meaning of the concept of gayness. While the term *joto* refers to the lower-class homosexual, which implies that the person will engage in a series of comparatively risky situations, a gay is a respectable person (Núñez Noriega 2005: 226–227). This anthropologist's observation suggests a cultural variation that distances itself from North American gay culture, assigning to gayness connotations of acculturation and even privilege, in contrast to conceptions of other homoerotic subjects (outside the realm of "gay") constituted by national traditions of homophobia. What Núñez Noriega calls euphemism consists of a translation of gayness by middle-class conformity, which from its privileged position no longer confronts homophobic violence because it is no longer experienced. Being gay, therefore, means maintaining an appearance and behavior that do not disturb dominant or mainstream society. This distancing from the victims of homophobia is evidence that being gay has taken on connotations of class prejudice and apathy that are contrary to its original activist concerns. I have witnessed, for example, how in the city of Guadalajara, Mexico, a large number of self-proclaimed gay men feel no solidarity with the transgender sex workers who were victims of violent attacks around 2006. They explained their position by stating that the physical assaults were not rooted in homophobia but rather in the fact that dressing as a transvestite is in itself an act of aggression toward society. This discriminatory statement is telling of the status of gayness

---

[6] *Joto* is a pejorative word for homosexuals; its most probable origin is the word *chotear*, which means "to scorn." *Chichifo* and *mayate* define the person who has the dominant role in homosexual contact (usually a prostitute); however, they are not considered homosexuals in traditional Mexican culture.

as a class marker and of transgender identity as secluded from mainstream LGBT politics.

Coming out: Recurring asymmetries

The incorporation in Latin American culture of a number of elements, involving politics and lifestyle, of American culture constitutes lessons of modernity, of which gay culture and politics is one of the most prominent. Among the lessons learned from the North American gay rights movement, Antonio Marquet (2001), a gay Mexican public intellectual and academic, underlines the act of coming out of the closet as a political phenomenon that has opened up spaces for sexual diversity. Two questions Marquet poses in regard to Kenneth Paul Rosenberg's documentary *Why Am I Gay?* (1993) point us to this enlightening reading: "Why doesn't the equivalent of Eddie Rodriguez, the New York policeman who declares his preferences to the camera in the middle of his precinct, exist in Mexico? Why can't the Mexican policeman quit being the jackal that besets, bribes, and violates the rights of homosexuals?" (Marquet 2001: 145–146). The questions formulated by Marquet introduce us to a comparative reading between the two judicial systems and activist practices. At the same time they indicate the best way of reading the relevant events of North American gay politics as actions exemplifying civic participation. We thus encounter a reiteration of one of the ways of interpreting North America legitimized by Mexican intellectuals: the exaltation of dissident subjects—the homage to North American civil society.

This exaltation of dissidents implies a criticism of the conservative aspect of the United States. In his note about the documentary *The Times of Harvey Milk* (1984), Marquet alludes to puritanism and intolerance as repudiated aspects of the image of North American society. The assassin of a gay politician from San Francisco is the pride of North American mothers in 1978 and represents the backward values of a dominant group characterized by a fundamentalist ideology (Marquet 2001: 140). Marquet concludes that this documentary shows how ethnic and sexual minorities, by joining together, can overcome the arbitrary rules of groups in power. This reading turns the North American gay rights sagas into instructional texts for the political practices of minorities.

According to Margaret Cruikshank (1992), the North American struggle for gay rights arose in the context of the hippie and civil rights peace movements. In her view, without this antiauthoritarian climate, which had developed a method of protest against the prejudices of North American society, the gay rights movement would not have emerged (62). Let us take this context as a point of comparison with the Mexican phenomenon. The 1968 student movement was the epitome of Mexican methods of political protest during the 1960s and beyond. In Mexico, neither civil rights nor peace were the focus of the protest. Rather, the movement was defined by demands for democracy and a clearly socialist agenda aligning Mexico more with the rest of Latin America than with the United States, where support for the socialist block did not enjoy the same popularity as civil rights and peace, at least in the 1960s through the 1980s. Within this context, it is important to remember that Latin American resistance in the 1960s was not articulated in terms of minority groups but rather was focused on protecting the nation and/or Latin American identity from North American domination: in other words, one was socialist because one was anti-United States.

Most scholars addressing sexual diversity issues have pointed out various levels of closeted sexuality in most Latin American regions (e.g., Decenas 2011; Núñez Noriega 1999, 2011; Quiroga 1999, 2000, 2010), where coming out is reserved for a privileged sector of gays. This is assumed to be the main contrast with American gay culture. Gay Latin Americans, because they are gay (if we understand gay to mean having gone through the initiation process of coming out), must generally leave the Catholic church (one of the most aggressively homophobic religious institutions) and break with their nuclear family—which can be understood as an extension of the church in its role as a creator and enforcer of moral codes. This fact leads us to consider how members of the Latin American gay population are more likely than those in the United States to live a double life.[7]

When speaking of the 1969 Stonewall riots in her essay "Gender in America," Drucilla Cornell (2004) said that "[t]he proclamation that one is gay and lesbian became as much a matter of ethical and political significance as of personal self-definition" (49). Thus, Cornell offers two concerns that define the gay rights movements: the ethical and political component and the individual act of self-definition. The first is characterized as an act of antihomophobic politics as well as an effort to ensure civil rights for those who identify as nonheteronormatively configured sexual subjects (which would be articulated with the creation and enforcement of laws that would equally benefit the nonheterosexual population). The aspect of self-definition can be understood as the creation of a space in the public sphere for the expression of these sexualities. For the North American movement, coming out of the closet is first and foremost a political act and therefore the organizing axis for gay ideology. Coming out of the closet fundamentally implies "taking on or assuming a condition ... but it also demands a certain degree of integration into the homosexual community" (Marquet 2001: 37, my translation).

In the introduction to his *Tropics of Desire: Interventions from Queer Latino America*, José Quiroga (2000) describes a tactic

---

[7] This does not mean that in the United States there are not cases of those who live a double life, as can be observed in the movie *Brokeback Mountain* (2005) and in the case of Pastor Ted Haggard of Colorado Springs, who resigned his post as president of the National Association of Evangelicals in November 2006 because he had been discovered to have had a homosexual relationship.

deployed in Buenos Aires' Gay Pride of 1993: the organizers distributed masks to those who wanted to march without being recognized. For Quiroga, "[t]he masks spoke of broader circuits that did not necessarily end with the 'outing', or an identity as conclusion" (1). Outing is not the objective, and thus identity, one of the main aspects of gay American politics, becomes only one item in a larger number of issues that inscribe LGBT demands among larger human rights struggles. The performance of wearing a mask makes evident that there is a society that can punish the scandal of outing; the mask is a defensive weapon in the fight against homophobia. In contrast to the individual rite of passage of coming out, masking the crowd collectivizes the demands of LGBT people and links them to the general resistance movement against homophobia. This point was underlined by the strategies Argentinean gay activist Carlos Jáuregui undertook: never to talk on behalf of a particular demand but always to keep in mind the broader social issues (Quiroga 2000: 4).

In North American gay activism, coming out of the closet is an act of public testimony—and thus a political act—that is a sign both of membership in a community and of self-definition, with all its accompanying social responsibilities and privileges. Many of my North American friends are perplexed when I describe the undefined nature of masculine sexuality in the majority of Latin American countries. For them one is or is not gay: identity is an act and an effect of identification and is presented unequivocally. This reflects one of the foundations of North American politics that grew out of the civil rights movements: the construction of identity or what has been called the politics of identity. This is a politics grounded on the idea of developing a political agenda for communities that have been oppressed because of race, sexuality, nationality, and so on. It is important to mention that it is precisely this politics of identity requiring self-definition that is questioned by queer theory: in short, this theory questions the essentialist constitution of sex and gender identity, proposing a view in which definition of the subject fluctuates. Does this mean that dissident sexualities in Latin America are more definable as queer than the American and European LGBT-identity-centered culture? And is that alleged Latin American queerness more liberating than LGBT politics?

In one of the most representative novels of Mexican gay literature, *El vampiro de la Colonia Roma* (The Vampire of the Colonia Roma) by Luis Zapata (1979), we can find what in Mexican homoerotic culture could be considered queer, though this culture resists the use of such tags. The protagonist, Adonis García, is a young prostitute whose relationships with clients lead him to experience all types of sexual contact. As he learns about new pleasures through these contacts, this character continually redefines his identity to the point that any stable definition is useless. Initially, Adonis is characterized as a *chichifo*, a type of man who practices homoeroticism as a means of subsistence and who only penetrates another man during specific homoerotic encounters; he therefore does not lose his prestige as a male and is considered heterosexual both by society and by himself. Ethnographers such as Marinella Miano Borruso (2003), Patricia Ponce (2001), and Anick Prieur (1998)locate this type (also called *mayate* or *chacal*) in the lower classes, in a field of sexual practices that are outside those characterized by gay culture. However, Adonis García (in his self-perception, if not in that of his clients) goes beyond the condition of *chichifo* and thus breaks out of the circle described by ethnography. Both the *chichifo* and the new character, located outside any identity that Adonis becomes, escape gay politics. The *chichifo* does not take on any specific political or social identity, nor does he belong to a community, and therefore he does not participate in the political practices that characterize gay activism. There has never existed, to my knowledge, any explicitly named group of *chichifos* in the pro-diversity marches in Mexico City.

The utopian proposal for sexuality expressed in *El vampiro de la Colonia Roma* suggests a contrast between North American gay concepts about identitarian definitions and Mexicans' stubborn resistance to categorization, at least with regard to defining identity as political performance in the former versus the inclination to live in the liminality of identities in the latter. In this novel, the public bathhouse, the most traditional and diverse space for homoerotic sexual encounters, is described as a community conceived and imagined on the basis of pleasure—that is to say, based on a consensus about the communal value ("communal" comes from "communion": sacred communication) of hedonism. It is from this point of view that the public bathhouse is described as a space of sexual democratization: "But there in the *Ecuador* [bathhouse] something very curious happens, that, well, there's a lot of cooperation between everyone, you see? As if everyone were equal there; sex wins out over social class, you know? And everyone cooperates so that everyone enjoys" (Zapata 1979: 201). Just as in the bathhouse, where a social desire for equality is outlined, where everyone worries about everyone else having an orgasm without making any distinctions of any kind, Adonis' body is a public good whose meaning comes from providing pleasure for others. This utopia of nondefined identities creates a paradise of sexuality where the ideological agency that organizes or gives meaning to Adonis' narrative can become transparent.

However, the direction followed by gay politics pursues a different form of democracy that points toward the official regulation of the gay couple: building identity and building community are, in the end, ways of continuing to build the state. This is an institutionalization of the politics of identity that is not possible without the commitment of coming out of the closet. This identity politics perspective is reflected in the various reforms in Latin America that have allowed same-sex marriage, which is institutionalized in order to protect assets and access to benefits. While Adonis' utopia contemplates the universal right to pleasure—a proposal that would be difficult to express in parliamentary spaces—the formalizing and legitimizing benefits of gay politics are evident in marriage initiatives in Argentina, Brazil, Chile, Colombia, Mexico, and Uruguay. The rights to pleasure and civic inclusion seem to be the two contradictory directions through which gayness gains significance. I am not contrasting North America and Latin America; rather, I am highlighting the contradictions that the presence of gayness produces in Latin American culture, contradictions that are in many ways a result of the Latin American perception and reception of US gayness, which is not quite equivalent to the history of the US queer movements.

The preoccupation with pleasure and the construction of identity remind us of one of the most important texts in relation to the contrast between the United States and Mexico: the essay "La mesa y el lecho" (The Table and the Bed), by Octavio Paz (1979). The exegesis that the Mexican intellectual makes of the table in order to explain the difference between the two countries can illuminate the distinction made here between the politics of pleasure and identity politics. Paz (1979) says, "North American cuisine is without mystery: simple ingredients, nutritional and lightly seasoned. No tricks: the carrot is the honorable carrot, the potato does not blush over its condition, and beef steak is a bloody giant" (215). While what Paz understands as North American cuisine has its reservations about "camouflaging sauces and dressings," in Mexican food "the secret is in the collision of flavors: fresh and spicy, salty and sweet, warm and acidic, sour and delicate. Desire is the active agent, the secret producer of changes, whether it has to do with the transition from one flavor to another or the contrast between several" (217). Without wishing to push the allegory too far, I find that this culinary speculation is useful for suggesting that the politics of coming out of the closet—that clear declaration that one belongs to a condition as honorable as the carrot and as shame-free as the potato—are uncomfortable for a culture that conceives of itself in ambiguous and contrasting terms of desire. Thus, the formative process of Mexican gay culture, and Latin American, for that matter, has fluctuated between the principles of identity (with the accompanying ethical demands of democratization) and the imperatives of pleasure—that hedonism so central to Paz's thought.

In his commentary on the theatrical production *Party* by David Dillon (1992), Antonio Marquet (2001) observes two characteristics of North American gay culture that are alien to Mexican culture and therefore practiced very little by that society's gays: the obsession with health and religious intervention. In this way the difference noted by Marquet is reminiscent of the pages Octavio Paz dedicates to comparing Mexican and North American cultures. For Marquet (2001), the party represented in Dillon's work "refuses to blossom in the chaotic liberty of spontaneity and contingency" (111). Marquet's observations echo Paz's comparison of the North American and Mexican parties in his essay "Todos santos, día de muertos" (All Saints, Day of the Death), in his *El laberinto de la soledad* (The Labyrinth of Solitude) (1950), while also focusing on one of the formational nuclei of gay identity: leisure. While the North American party is governed by rules that protect the integrity of the event, the Mexican party risks excess.

In James Green's *Beyond Carnival* (1999) it is clear that gay politics is enacted in the carnival, legitimizing itself through the seduction of the excess and the *jouissance* of the mob. Activists in Rio de Janeiro explain to Rafael de la Dehesa (2010) that the first LGBT marches in that city were unsuccessful because marches did not make sense to Brazilians, as they were used to carnival (199). It is telling that most of the chronicles describing homosexual life and struggles in Latin America are related to nightclubs, private parties, and bathhouses, and to the violent intrusion of the police to repress and arrest sexual dissidents. In his *De los baños a la calle* (From Bathhouses to the Street), Uruguayan historian Diego Sempol (2013) refers to a case that illustrates the intrusion of the state in a private party. The police arrived at a country house, where about 300 lesbians and homosexuals, some of them cross-dressed, were celebrating a birthday. Seventy-one of them were detained for six days, but also they lost jobs, were banned from attending schools, and suffered exclusion from social circles (Sempol 2013: 28–29). Pleasure seems to be the main infraction the state is trying to punish. In some countries of the region (such as Nicaragua), sodomy was banned until the twenty-first century, and in many Latin American cities the police still repress gay gatherings arguing that they represent a moral scandal. The fear of losing its filiation to society or being unprotected from homophobia means that in Peru, for instance, the LGBT movement is precarious (Cuba 2012: 18–19).[8] Homophobia—rather than coming out and the institutionalization of LGBT privileges—has been the main target of Latin American LGBT activism.

Homophobia: The capital cause

To what degree have the lessons of the United States' civil rights struggles, specifically those of the LGBT movement, prospered in Latin America? While activism has been remarkably effective in the area of legislation against discrimination and homophobia, and public opinion in favor of rights such as marriage is advancing in many countries, official and social homophobia, and mainly transphobia, is still a hard reality faced by LGBT communities. Argentina and Uruguay are exceptions in having a low incidence of violence; in other countries, sexual diversity faces setbacks in

---

[8] Thanks to activists and writers Violeta Barrientos and Sara Rondinel for their valuable information on LGBT issues in Peru.

the area of human rights, where, as in the case of women and indigenous peoples, the situation has not only become worse but even lethal.[9] Many instances of homophobic violence around the continent are evidence of this worsening situation. Indeed, the region has the highest number of reported homophobic murders (Brazil, Mexico, and the United States are the most murderous countries for homosexuals in the world, in that order). In Brazil, it has been hard to advance legislation against discrimination and hate crime.

The difficulties of reporting hate crimes in Latin America hinder the knowledge of how extended this specific form of violence is. Nevertheless, it is telling that the two most populous countries in the region have the largest number of homophobic crimes in the world. Grupo Gay da Bahía (Gay Group of Bahía) reports that every twenty-six hours a hate crime is committed in Brazil (Rodgers 2013). In the case of Mexico, the Comisión Ciudadana contra los Crímenes de Odio por Homofobia (Citizens' Commission against Homophobic Hate Crimes) calculates that there is on average one hate crime every other day (*Télam* 2013). Alejandro Brito, one of the most renowned activists for LGBT rights, asserts that, after the approval of same-sex marriage in Mexico City, homophobic hate crimes increased in number (*Télam* 2013). Lawrence La Fountain-Stokes (2014) explains the murder of Jorge Stevens López Mercado in 2009, in Puerto Rico, as a backlash against the legislative and cultural success of the LGBT community (136). In Brazil, the

---

[9] Salvador and Honduras are the countries with the highest annual rate of femicides in the world, with 15 and 14 murders per 100,000 habitants respectively; between 2011 and 2015 Mexico's annual femicide rate increased from 2.4 to 3.2 murders per 100,000 habitants (Geneva Declaration on Armed Violence and Development 2015). Mine and oil companies are dispossessing indigenous communities from their territories and reducing their possibility of surviving. Countries with large indigenous populations, such as Brazil, Mexico, and Peru, have experienced numerous conflicts between state actors, transnational companies, and native nations (Ahmadov and Guliyev 2016; De la Cuadra 2015).

country with the highest reported number of homophobic murders in the world, after the LGBT organizations started to lobby the National Congress to advance rights relating to sexual diversity, churches reacted with an intense participation in legislature to the point of forming a strong bloc against pro-LGBT bills. But, as Rafael de la Dehesa (2010) notes, appeals to the Supreme Court have been an effective way to establish jurisprudence, opening the way for the increase of rights for sexual dissidents (125–131). This was the route taken by same-sex marriage, which is legal in Brazil thanks to the National Justice Council's decision.

It seems like the countries with more hate crimes are those that have been more prominent in their LGBT activism (Brazil, Mexico, and the United States). But this assertion is not applicable to Argentina and Uruguay, where LGBT rights are more advanced than in the rest of the region and the homophobic murder rate is low. Thus, while the number of reported hate crimes in Brazil was more than 300 in 2014 and while in Mexico there is an average of seventy homophobically motivated murders per year, in Argentina only five cases were reported in 2013 (Grupo Gay da Bahía 2015; *Letra Ese* 2015). In an interview I conducted in July 2012, Esteban Paulón, president of the Federación Argentina de Lesbianas, Gays, Bisexuales, y Trans (Argentine Federation of Lesbians, Gays, and Transsexuals), explained that the very small participation of the evangelical churches in Argentina's Congress was a key factor in its easy passage of the equal marriage proposal. Nevertheless, for Argentinean sociologist Daniel Jones (2008), that homophobia is presented as comparatively rare in Argentina is mainly propaganda aiming to promote the idea of a modern and civilized country. Indeed, in his work on stigmatization and discrimination against gay adolescents in Trelew, a small city in the Patagonia region, Jones (2008) argues that, while Buenos Aires has become a gay-friendly place, the province is as homophobic as the rest of the continent (51). This conflicting picture shows that law reforms do not imply immediate cultural changes. These facts oblige us to delve into the systems, the organizational practices, and the contexts that influence the failure of policies in one region that were successful in the other. The analysis of this lack of success will be a key task for conducting a gay politics that resignifies the global LGBT agenda.

Among the Mexican immigrant population in Colorado, I have found that one of the reasons for gay Mexicans to migrate was being able to publically admit their homosexuality, which implies that when they go home they go back into the closet. A few years ago, I spoke with a gay activist in Mexico City who, when he was going to visit his family in a mountain town in Puebla, was worried because he had been interviewed by one of the newscasts with the widest national coverage in the country and he was afraid of facing the disapproval of his compatriots. Does this mean that the Mexican gay rights movement is only half finished because it has not been able to find a political solution to the problem of complete visibility, which is considered essential to achieving social acceptance? Is "coming out of the closet" an obligatory part of the definition of "gay" or is it enough to take on an identity and live with the community intermittently, without the need for exhibitionism? Should the concept of gay identity be redefined, to the extent that cultural conditions in Latin America are neither favorable to—nor prone to—developing the North American form of gay politics?

Porfirio Hernández Cabrera (2005) mentions that among the factors that broke up the Centro para la Liberación Sexual (Center for Sexual Liberation) in Mexico was that the "inability to achieve support from the community when coming out of the closet was imposed as the only form of 'liberation'" (292, my translation). The difficulty of coming out of the closet and associating with the homosexual community in most areas of Latin America necessarily creates scenarios in which it is possible to come out whenever it is necessary. Everyday life for many LGBT people is lived, one could say, "in the closet," and it is only when they return to the community of other homosexuals that they "come out." Paradoxically, the open space implies being "closeted" while the gay community (where one "comes out") is found in closed, exclusive, and often stigmatized environments. It can be said that in Latin America in general one does not expose oneself definitively: one goes in and comes out according to the precodified use of spaces. In Costa Rica, any conduct in public spaces that can be interpreted as gay cruising is enough for the police to take disciplinary action, restricting homoerotic expressions to nightclubs and private spaces. In Mexico City, middle-class neighborhoods and tourist areas are safe zones for expressing same-sex affection, but the most lower-class areas are not tolerant at all. The same can be said of Buenos Aires, Argentina, and Santiago, Chile. A large number of gays from rural settings travel frequently to cities in order to come out temporarily. In his ethnographic study of the homosexual population in western Mexico, Joseph Carrier (2002) tells how men from the countryside make special weekend trips to the city to engage in sexual acts with other men (40–41). "Sexilio," as Puerto Rican sociologist Manolo Guzmán (1997) calls it, is the exile of those who have to flee their community because of their sexual orientation (227). In an analysis of sexiles from Latin America to the United States and Canada, Norma Mogrovejo (2016) points out that sexilio makes apparent the state of exception with respect to sexual minorities in the region, despite the great advancement in legislative reforms championing LGBT rights (242). But also, for her, it is a subtle way to reaffirm the superiority of the northern countries as paradises of human rights, a pretention that is disavowed when we remember that the United States has the third highest rate of reported hate crimes (Morgrovejo 2016: 243). Yolanda Martínez-San Miguel (2011) goes beyond this national-empire framework by distinguishing sexilio as expulsion from sexilio as a process of cultural negotiation where the patriarchal basis of the national imaginary is put in crisis by Caribbean authors writing about sexilio while being in sexilio (26). Coming out is not only a personal decision that establishes one's gay identity but also a counternational political action, as sexilio means not only a defensive decision but also a proactive challenge to the whole system, which overlaps patriarchal and nationalistic ideologies. Lawrence La Fountain-Stokes (2009: 132–133) finds that the center of Nuyorican culture,[10] the culture of the Puerto Rican diaspora, is located in the Bronx, as a queer utopia where all differences are welcomed; this utopia displaced the heteronormative, macho, nationalistic structure of power for a multicultural, queer cultural scene. This means that what La Fountain-Stokes places at the center of Nuyorican culture is the stage and art scene of the Bronx. This approach is reminiscent of Jose E. Muñoz's (2009) utopian locus of queer politics: the performance as the art of historical anticipation (4). For Muñoz, queerness is not something we can find in the concrete world but a project of what is not yet in place. That sense of a work in process—the impulse of going beyond ready-made identities (a ready-made that can be perceived as a colonizing, alienating imposition of definitions and practices)—will be discussed in Chapter 4.

The AIDS pandemic

In spite of the leadership crisis in the first era of the LGBT movement in Latin America, various groups arose during the 1980s, in reaction in particular to the huge shock that the AIDS pandemic sent through the homosexual population. This revival of the LGBT movement reiterated the global nature of gay activism—a global nature that owes less to militancy and ideological propaganda and more to emerging situations in a community that has come together as a result of exclusion, threats, and multiple forms of oppression.

---

[10] "Nuyorican" is a portmanteau that combines "New York" with "Puerto Rican."

In their book *Empire* (2000), Michael Hardt and Antonio Negri observe that social movements in the era of globalization tend to be immediate in nature, arising in response to emerging situations. Thus, what can be spoken of as a globalized movement does not owe as much to a priori political projects as it does to contingencies that arise at the international level: it is not so much political discourse that is globalized as it is the phenomena that trigger the surge of spontaneous social movements (Hardt and Negri 2000: 52–56). The AIDS pandemic acted as one of the political triggers of global activism and was analyzed by Hardt and Negri. Another factor that stimulated the emergence of a global gay rights movement was the need for international politics that responded to growing conservatism. This political emergence became a more and more firmly established presence in the arts, media, and academia, though it was not a projected political agenda but rather a plural response to conservative pressure. Mexican scholar and activist Gloria Careaga (2005) points out that political proposals about sexuality have reached international academic and professional forums capable of making recommendations to governments about local legislation in favor of minority human rights. These recommendations have provoked aggressive responses from Catholic, Muslim, and Orthodox Christian hierarchies, which have undertaken hostile erotic-phobic, antiabortion, and homophobic campaigns. Local movements have then articulated positions in favor of the recommendations made in these global forums and against the attacks from conservative groups. In this way, gay regional politics became oriented toward bringing to fruition the implied promises governments made with the adoption of these international recommendations (Careaga 2005: 311).

As a result of the AIDS pandemic, instead of taking legislative avenues to promote the LGBT agenda, activists used health offices to process their demands relating to HIV, stigmatization, prevention, and treatments. According to Rafael de la Dehesa (2010), in the

1990s, under the pressure of increasing discrimination and official homophobia, the sexual diversity cause was revitalized in Brazil and Mexico. Groups worked in coalitions and nongovernmental organizations entered the political scene, providing services that before had been exclusively provided by the state (de la Dehesa 2010: 154–155).

AIDS brought biases and stigmas to the public conversation, making the search for health and social survival difficult for infected individuals. Negative stereotypes changed identities and increased homophobia in the 1980s and 1990s. Literary critic Jodie Parys (2012) notes that, in Latin America, literary production very seldom referred to the disease (and when it did it was in a biased fashion) while the pandemic advanced, wreaking havoc in homosexual populations (7–8).

Homophobia made the illness additionally dangerous. In her study of the stigmatization of HIV carriers in Veracruz, Mexico, Rosa María Lara y Mateos (2006) asserts that homophobia is the greatest health problem in this city and has contributed to the city having the highest rate of HIV infection in the country (20). Because of stigmatization, there is a lack of attention in academic research to male HIV infection in this region, despite the fact that this is the most affected population (51). Indeed, as Héctor Carrillo (2002) asserts, in the 1980s in Mexico, journalists presented AIDS using biased language; officials downplayed the gravity of the disease, and even health professionals refused to attend infected people. It was only when community groups started to take action against this environment in 1986 that authorities took the pandemic seriously (Carrillo 2002: 214). But this pressure was not the only factor responsible for the change of public policy with respect to HIV–AIDS. In the early 1990s the Pan American Health Organization asked governments of the continent "to establish national AIDS councils that would administer international prevention funds channeled through its AIDS programs" (Carrillo 2002: 216). Rafael de la Dehesa (2010) notes that similar international pressures made the Brazilian government implement HIV–AIDS-related actions. From 1994 to 1998 the World Bank issued a loan to establish the STD Control Project; since then, every new loan to Brazil has been used on a new version of the AIDS project (de la Dehesa 2010: 182).

HIV–AIDS unleashed a virulent conservative campaign against sexual practice and encouraged condemnation of homosexuals. The efforts to disseminate information in order prevent the spread of HIV in the 1990s were sabotaged by the Catholic organizations in Guadalajara, Mexico; these organizations invested all of their resources in prohibiting public education about prophylactic measures, arguing that they promote promiscuity (Carrillo 2002: 223–224). In a similar context, Osvaldo Bazán (2004) notes that in Argentina in the late 1980s, people commonly considered sodomy to be the cause of AIDS (409–411). These local disputes between LGBT organizations and the powerful conservative sectors defined the route that sexual diversity politics would follow up to the present. The official position is enacted under the pressure of external actors such as the World Bank and the international organizations, but the most conservative forces also deploy their influence in sexual matters. LGBT issues became, then, a key aspect of the human rights agenda, and the discourses of identity and liberation were replaced by discourses of rights and public policies. In his analysis of the design and implementation of an antihomophobia media campaign in Mexico, Jordi Díez (2010) emphasizes the use of scientific and human rights frameworks in the public debate against the conservative arguments that were influential in the Vicente Fox regime (33).

AIDS transmission in Latin America unveiled a more complex sexual culture than that of Western Europe and the United States. While the homosexual sector was identified as a high-risk population in the latter countries, a very different sexual culture in Latin American countries, where the binary opposition homosexual–

heterosexual is blurred, demanded a distinct approach to prevention and treatment of the disease. According to Richard Parker (1999), in Brazil stigmatization is applied to passive participants in homosexual intercourse, whereas active (top) participants retain macho privileges; thus, the latter are not deemed to be part of the population at risk, because they are not perceived as *viado* or *bicha*, the derogatory terms for effeminate men. This is the case because practices and identities do not correspond to each other. Sexuality observes a fluid behavior while sexual identities work in the field of social relations. In the case of Brazil, Parker (1999) asserts, sexuality happens in a hidden, undifferentiated space, where everything can happen and there is no need to define it (257–258).

Joseph Carrier (2002) estimates that about 30 percent of Mexican men have experienced sexual contact with other men (81). Guillermo Núñez Noriega (1999) considers Carrier's guess to be conservative, based on his own ethnography in Hermosillo, Mexico (208). Annick Prieur (1998) asserts that bisexuality is more widespread in Mexico than in the United States or Europe. One of her informants conducted his own census, counting thirty neighboring households in Ciudad Neza, a populous sector in the Mexico City metropolitan area, and concluded that in his neighborhood 63 percent of men had had sex with another man (180).

As invisible as it is widespread, bisexuality in Latin America constituted a challenge to the implementation of AIDS-prevention public policies. The concept "MSM," or men who have sex with men, was put into circulation in order to destigmatize the disease by unlinking it from any identity—MSM was just the category most affected by the virus. Bisexuality caused an emergency, stalling the prevention and diagnosis of AIDS among the population most likely to be infected: men who, despite their homoerotic practices, reject being identified as homosexual (Sívori 2004: 263–265).

The homo–bisexual population was the group with the largest number of HIV infections in 1990s Cuba. Statistics show that Cuba was the most successful country in controlling the disease, although the initial methods in the 1980s of mandatory quarantine in total isolation were subject to criticism by Latin American artists and intellectuals. The Chilean writer Pedro Lemebel, for instance, in his chronicle "El fugado de la Habana" (The Escaped of Habana), makes clear the state of segregation and persecution experienced by the HIV bearers. In his visit to this city, Lemebel met a young artist who lived with fear of being arrested and forced to be reinterned in the sanatorium from where he had managed to escape years before (Lemebel 2000: 159–165). In the film *Azúcar Amarga* (Bitter Sugar) (1996), directed by Cuban American filmmaker León Ichaso, the character Bobby, the black sheep of a socialism-supporting family, is tired of the police's constant repression of his heavy rock band and decides with other friends to inject HIV-infected blood into himself. Days after this decision, the police forcefully enter his apartment, arrest him, and take him to a quarantine sanatorium. According to Liana Rodríguez Roch (1997), the quarantine was a determinant in the fact that a low propagation of the Cuban population was infected with HIV (132). But the method of mandatory reclusion and subsequent stigmatization were questionable in terms of the human rights of patients.

Normalizing the queer

There is a contradiction between, on the one hand, the definition of queer as nonconformity to the rules of gender and sexuality and, on the other, the politics of same-sex marriage. If marriage is one of the most powerful institutions for patriarchal control, according to the feminist and sexual liberation movements (a position that was embraced by the LGBT movement of the 1970s and 1980s), we can say that the LGBT movement today has renounced liberation politics in order to emphasize a politics of rights. The former (liberation politics) was the consequence of an overarchingly Marxist ideology regarding resistance movements in Latin America during the Cold War, with these movements' revolutionary program consisting of the overturning of the capitalist system in order to install a new socialist order, where, accordingly, the transformation of the gender system would be a natural consequence—at least in the statements of Marxist, feminist, and LGBT activists. The latter (the politics of rights) coincided, first, with the end of the Cold War and the beginning of neoliberalism as a dominant political and economic system, and, second, with the emergence of AIDS, which, as a public concern (because of its pandemic nature) and as a disease that disproportionately affected the homosexual population, placed homosexuality in a privileged position in public policies. LGBT activism, instead of confronting the institutions (as required by revolutionary socialism), approached them, arguing that controlling the disease required fighting homophobia. The civil rights movement, like LGBT activism, is oriented primarily toward the inclusion of the marginalized and disenfranchised, which implies extending citizenship to those sectors that have been oppressed. But extending the rights of the majority to the minority can be conceived as erasing difference. Being a beneficiary of specific public policies designed primarily to benefit sexual diversity and being one of the targeted populations for human rights initiatives in the international arena, LGBT politics has had important achievements in the public sphere since the 1990s. These achievements have placed sexual diversity on an integrative path that is contrary to its initial revolutionary politics, its original countersocial impulse (Mogrovejo 2011: 235).

Same-sex marriage and the availability of gender identity reassignment have been the ultimate achievements of the LGBT movement. Nevertheless, various actors coming from the most liberal fronts (LGBT, feminist, leftist, and decolonial academics and activists) perceive this egalitarian legal reform not as an advancement but as a step backward. Uruguayan historian Diego Sempol (2013) summarizes the arguments of this opposition in the following terms: state regulation of same-sex unions implies assimilation of sexual dissidence to state control; it means the imposition of heteronormative models on sexual diversity; it only reproduces traditional roles; and it disregards the concept that marriage is a form of violence. On the other hand, those who favor same-sex civil unions argue that they redefine social norms and break prejudices and that they also have a more practical benefit: providing rights that protect patrimony, facilitating adoption of children by same-sex couples, and providing partner benefits that were previously exclusive to heterosexuals. Sempol (2013) proposes that we should understand the implementation of this reform in terms of the needs that originated it and the practical issues that it resolves for the LGBT community (389–391).

The LGBT movement is distanced not only from the revolutionary approach but also from the feminist agenda. Marriage is a patriarchal institution that for centuries has enslaved women in terms of unpaid domestic work, mandatory maternity and monogamy, and domestic violence. Mexican intellectual Gabriel Zaid (2015) expresses his disagreement with same-sex marriage, lamenting a backward trend in the route of liberation that can be traced back to the second century. According to this posture, the antimarriage position is part of a tradition of sequential ruptures that defines modernity for liberal intellectuals such as the Mexican Nobel laureate Octavio Paz. From this liberal perspective, feminist struggles are considered as one of the most radical proposals of the revolutionary episteme. Marriage, the most consolidated of the patriarchal institutions, is one of the main targets of feminist ideology.

Feminist and liberal opposition to same-sex marriage have converged with the Catholic church's mobilizations against social policy. The questions that marriage unleashes go beyond the issue of marriage itself: if it is called equal marriage, is it a form of destabilizing patriarchy or a renunciation of the fight against patriarchy? Is this a way of debilitating sex–gender causes in the context of increasing conservatism in present times? Would it be a symptom of dismantling the liberation ideology that has nurtured modernity and therefore a definitive dismounting of modern ways of thinking and acting? Is it a strategy for demobilizing LGBT fights by incorporating sexual diversity into the standards of the establishment? Are the rights of LGBT people necessarily a threat to the rights of women?

The fact that the Catholic church in Mexico and the Evangelical churches in Brazil have been prominent in the opposition to same-sex marriage is by itself a reason for a liberation politics. But in what way can it be a threat to the patriarchal, religion-supported system of the control of bodies? While sexual dissidents were expected to be invisible and disenfranchised, in the marginal spaces assigned to them by the dominant, homophobic, Catholic society, same-sex marriage marks the admittance of the sexual dissident in the field of rights and citizenship—that is, the abolition of the heterosexual–homosexual divide as a device of discrimination. For intellectuals such as Mogrovejo and Zaid (2015), this integrative process is consolidating, instead of dismantling, the very patriarchal institution of bodily control. Does it mean that same-sex marriage marks the end of dissidence in LGBT politics? If the political, according to French philosopher Jacques Rancière (2010), is distinguished for its dissenting character, when marriage normalizes the difference, under the principle of equality the politics of sexual dissidence is no longer oppositional. The oppositional character of LGBT politics, however, is not cancelled until homophobic politics is extinguished. Same-sex marriage could be just a good signal that the politics of sexual dissidence is getting good results.

The transformation of the liberation discourse into one of rights that de la Dehesa (2010) points out can be understood, according to Jordi Díez (2015), in relation to the change of political strategy that emerged in the midst of the emergency caused by the AIDS pandemic. This strategy consists of the professionalization of activism, the application of policy frameworks structured by scientific research, and the use of media technologies to fight in the field of policymaking. In fact, same-sex marriage is a public policy that expands the scope of citizenship and that reinforces the state, far from destabilizing or overturning it.

On the other hand, same-sex marriage can be seen as an achievement that is the pinnacle of the process started in the 1960s and not necessarily as a significant departure from the former liberation epistemology, as it is an advancement rather than a backward step for the goal of gaining full citizenship for the LGBT community. By taking the role of policymakers, sexual diversity activists are working from inside the institutions rather than confronting them. This argument also has to do with the institutionalization of the left in the 1990s and 2000s. In the Cold War period, the left and its LGBT allies were positioned against the state; now, with the re-establishing of democracy in various countries in South America, the left and LGBT groups are part of the state and have an important role in policymaking. Same-sex marriage is understood as the assimilation of the difference and thus its cancellation. But it is also a form of queering the state, where the normalization of the queer is also a depriveleging of the heteronormative.

In an interview given in 2001, the Chilean writer and public intellectual Pedro Lemebel declared that he would stop his activism in favor of sexual diversity when sexual dissidents were no longer conflicting with law and society—meaning when stigmas about difference are totally extinguished (Lemebel 2013). This assertion suggests that fighting stigma is not necessarily about removing difference but rather about its rejection or marginalization. Arguably, the LGBT movement would culminate at the point this rejection or marginalization was achieved.

CHAPTER 4

Beyond LGBT struggles: Trans politics and neoliberal sex

This chapter addresses cultural and political expressions that emerged on the margins of mainstream LGBT interests. Beyond the agendas of liberation and rights of gays and lesbians, stigmatizations and discriminations motivate resistant political identities, whose diverse expressions in the public sphere allow us to think on queer Latin American culture as a source of novel proposals of subjectivities that challenge the cultural and political establishment. Such is the case with the transsexual, transgender, and intersex groups, whose expressions demand identity recognition, as a specific gender delimitation, in contrast to the heterosexism expressed in laws and social codes. The trans identity challenges the very foundations of the gender system, and this terror can trigger fierce homophobic crimes. But, in their struggle, the trans not only demand recognition but also criticize the heteronormative political system. The trans identity is one of the most dynamic stages from which to "queer" the hegemonic culture. In this chapter I discuss how trans subjects have intervened in the public sphere but also how market forces have recolonized queerness, finding in the representations of subaltern queer bodies new challenges to queer politics. This means the subaltern, or the monster that has been secluded to the margin, can finally speak. It is the monster that tells a political truth that necessarily takes the public discussion to the matter of the body as a field of ideological disputes. Jeffrey Jerome Cohen (1996: 4) reminds us that the monster reveals and warns—prophetic actions that can be traced back to the oracles of ancient Greece and the dements referred to in Michel Foucault's *History of Madness* (2006: 210).

But, on the other hand, corporeal practices also have to be understood in the context of neoliberal colonial oppression of peripheral bodies. To objectify the colonized body is to alienate it in favor of the colonizing order of meaning. This is the zone of bodies that are troubled as result of colonization. In this chapter, I aim to discuss the mechanism by which the queer subject in the colonial and modern systems becomes a monster to be feared and punished, a scapegoat that has to be sacrificed or otherwise has to be resignified as bodily merchandise in the context of a neoliberal economy. The consumption of the colonial body as a commodity in the present times re-enacts the colonization of the native. The peripheral neoliberal environment has to be understood as the emergence of underground queer job markets for the unemployed masses serving global tourism. The objectification of the body, its production (meaning the process of becoming a product), and its consumption constitute new forms of slavery and the disposability of the body—issues that queer academic conversations, activism, and the arts are addressing as their new challenges for reflection and action.

Trans talk

Several instances on the continent show that gay and lesbian mainstream agendas differ from and sometimes ignore those of trans and intersex populations. While same-sex civil unions have gradually been legalized in Argentine cities and provinces (Buenos Aires, 2002; Río Negro, 2003; Villa Carlos Paz, 2009; etc.), police practices of extortion and blackmailing against transgender sex workers, and the ambiguity in the city ordinances regarding this population, are prevalent on the streets of Buenos Aires, and the trans community still has to endure incarceration and harassment by officials (Fernández 2005: 39–40). As Josefina Fernández (2005) exposes in her review of police violence against transgender sex workers in Buenos Aires, trans activism is reactive to official abuses; that is why human rights violations are at the core of the trans political discourse. For Carlos Figari (2014), trans and intersex social militancy centers on the question of gender, as the recognition of their trans identity by the law means for them the possibility of achieving full citizenship (67). The politics of the trans constitutes a specific chapter of the LGBT movement, but often it is manifested independently from gay and lesbian mainstream activism. By denouncing concrete human rights violations in their political performance interventions and by creating visual and documental archives, the trans community has been present in the public sphere, which has radically questioned the gender system altogether.

Chilean filmmaker Gloria Camiruaga's *Casa particular* (1989) is a short film that documents the community of the trans brothel called Casa Particular located on San Camilo Street, in the capital Santiago. Camiruaga's camera captures the underground scene of sex service for the macho conservative working class. The sex workers' stories tell the tragedy of their fellow workers who have died. The documentary uses Christian metaphors, exhibiting the victimization of the trans body in terms of sacrifice. The presence among the sex workers of the performers Pedro Lemebel and Francisco Casas (forming the duet "Las Yeguas del Apocalipsis" (The Mares of the Apocalypse)) connects this film with the several performances this duet presented in various public spaces in Chile during the dictatorship of Augusto Pinochet (1973–1990) and the postdictatorship period. The trans body articulates a demand to be recognized as part of the nation, a citizen with complete rights, but also intersects with the larger political arena of democracy and demands for human rights.

In Pedro Lemebel's performance and literature, the figure of the transgender reaches a heroic status: she collaborates in the resistance against Pinochet in his novel *Tengo miedo torero* (My Tender Matador) (2001). In an interview I had with her in 2002, Chilean poet and activist Gloria Thiers referred to the same period Lemebel fictionalizes in this novel. She was part of the Frente Patriótico Manuel Rodríguez (Patriotic Front Manuel Rodríguez), a clandestine communist armed group that attempted an assassination of Pinochet in 1986. In this pro-guerrilla resistance movement, Thiers stated, "the presence of women and queer people was the determining factor" (my translation). Clandestine radio station Radio Tierra and feminist organization La Morada (The Dwelling) were two of the most influential resistance fronts, and the gender and sexual diversity agendas were the most promoted.

The political intervention of the transgender is present in several narratives around the continent, beginning with the revolutionary novels by Mexican novelist José Rubén Romero. In his novel *Apuntes de un lugareño* (Notes by a Local) (1964), with all his womanly mannerisms, Gabino, a transvestite, delivers harangues of insurrection (54). Transgender heroes are also represented as transmasculine subjects. *La negra Angustias* (The Black Angustias) by Francisco Rojas González narrates the story of Colonel Angustias, a fictionalization of Colonel Amelio Robles, a famous revolutionary and Emiliano Zapata's subaltern who was born Amelia Robles and was finally recognized as a military male by the Mexican government (Cano 1999: 25). Trans subjects are prevalent in political narratives, where the cross-dressed character lives a form of romance with the rebel or is the transgender man, who occupies the position of the leader, as mentioned before in works by authors such as Manuel Puig and Pedro Lemebel. But these cases of transgender individuals of heroic narratives are not the only way the trans subject is present in the public arena. They fight to legalize the reassignation of gender and have made possible specific policies.

Even though narratives of transphobia can be counted among the cruelest stories regarding sex–gender violence, transgender activists have developed unique tactics of resistance toward abuses by authorities and criminals. In 2009, amid the crudest period of violence in Ciudad Juárez, Mexico, a group of trans sex workers were often victims of extortion by the police and criminals. They conceived a system of alerts that included whistles, codes, and simultaneous messaging of activists and journalist networks that would within minutes bring people to the place where abuse was to happen.[1]

In an interview I conducted with drag performer Alejandra Rodríguez in Ciudad Juárez, Mexico, in 2000, Rodríguez detailed the difficulties of dealing with police extortion and the hostility she experienced from people in the city. Her daily life had to be restricted to the red light district to enable her to feel safe. She had to negotiate her existence with her family, the community, and the police. Her show was appreciated not only by a gay audience but also by heterosexuals, when she was invited to their private celebrations. In her opinion, people in general were amazed at how it was possible for a man to transform into such a beautiful woman. For Rodríguez, it was an achievement that in becoming a woman she had seduced people to admire her beauty instead of insulting her.

In his book *Transvestism, Masculinity, and Latin American Literature*, Ben Sifuentes-Jáuregui (2002) sees the performativity

---

[1] This information comes from my own field work notes.

of transvestism as a gendering counterculture that constitutes a queer politics in Latin America. If cross-dressing is a political practice, it is not in the ideological sense of developing a program against the establishment through Manichean extrapolation. The politics of the body is concealed within the action of creating a challenging appearance and is articulated in that appearance's visual deployment (3).

In the chapter "Gender without Limits: The Erotics of Masculinity in *El lugar sin límites*," Sifuentes-Jáuregui emphasizes the gender indeterminacy that transvestism involves. In her/his cross-dressing, la Manuela—the protagonist of the Chilean author José Donoso's novel *El lugar sin límites* (A Place without Limits) (1966)—not only becomes an emulation of a woman but also crosses incessantly from the masculine to the feminine, from an effeminate masculinity to a masculinized femininity. S/he is raped because of his disturbing virility; s/he is desired and rejected at the same time because of her effeminacy. Sifuentes-Jáuregui points out that the transvestite represents a fundamental danger to heterosexuality. La Manuela is killed not because of his/her performance, which is celebrated as the main stage event in the little town of Southern Chile, but because of the menace transvestism implies to the seduced heterosexual.

While transvestism might be about the manipulation of the surfaces and appearances of gender expression, it is not a soft and trivial affair. The radical politics of transvestism goes to the root of the symbolic system that supports the whole of patriarchal hierarchy; transvestism's logic distrusts the discourse of the authentic, of the natural, and of unquestionable essentialisms. As Sifuentes-Jáuregui writes about the Cuban novelist Severo Sarduy (1982) (whose figurations are mainly concerned with cross-dressing's performativity, its "mask," and its destabilization of subjectivity), "the transvestite's subjectivity is (ac)claimed by showing the illegitimate claims of naturalness of the 'original': the very event of transvestism is not simply mimesis, but a performance that calls into question the performance of the original" (130). Through his/her multilayered parody, the transvestite calls into question the authenticity of gender, showing that the performance of the heteronormative is also transvestism.

Most trans politics happens on the stage, where trans have been both admitted and rejected, but this arena has finally been established as one of the most radical forums in the Latin American metropolis. From popular circus and nightclubs to middle-class cabaret theater, the drag character is the protagonist in sex talk that is also a political diatribe in which seduction and harangue, sensuality and caricature are intertwined. The fascination with the trans dressed as a seducer of machos is a leitmotif in Latin American literature. She inflames passion in hypermasculine characters—as in *El lugar sin límites* and Fernando Zamora's *Por debajo del agua* (Under the Water) (2002)—but she also becomes the voice of the tribe, a sort of Sybil who conveys political opinion through cabaret theater and circus spectacles, articulated from the queer point of view (examples include César Enríquez Cabaret and Tito Vasconcelos in Mexico and Circus Timoteo in Chile).

In 2002, thanks to the writer and activist Juan Pablo Sutherland, I had the opportunity to visit the Circus Timoteo in Santiago, Chile. I had read Pedro Lemebel's (1997) chronicle on this spectacle and was attracted to the idea of a circus where the host and the clown were a group of transgender women who previously used to be performers in nightclub drag shows (93–97). The show was dominated by homophobic insults from the public and clever responses from the drag clowns. Comic exchange becomes a political arena when the exposition of the weakness of the macho seems to be the goal of the transgender performer.

This kind of joke-based challenge to the public is part of the drag show genre, which in Mexico is called *perreo* or "bitchy talk." This challenge can also be a means of perpetuating homophobia, as can be seen in several drag shows in Mexico City, where the gay public is constantly accused of being a bottom (dominated or passive position in homoerotic sexual relations) or feminine as a form of denigration. In the case of Las hermanas vampiro (The Vampire Sisters), a drag show of the Zona Rosa district in Mexico City, insulting the audience is the source of laughter. The gender talk of drag aligns to the macho-centered culture by establishing the feminine as derogatory and the macho figure as the object of attraction. In the night club Spartacus, a popular drag queen discotheque on the outskirts of Mexico City, the sector that represents the macho audience, identified as *mayate* (a man who does not identify himself as homosexual and plays the dominant role in his sexual contact with effeminate homosexuals) is not the target of attacks; instead, *mayates* are constantly presented as desirable men. The drag show becomes an exaltation of the *mayate*, the figure of the macho, or an exaggeration of the macho performance. As I have explained in another work, the *mayate*'s sexuality is motivated by his wish to be recognized as macho in effeminate men's eyes (Domínguez Ruvalcaba 2007: 136–137). In his ethnography on transgender sex services in Colima, Mexico, César O. González Pérez (2003) describes *mayates* as working-class, scruffy individuals who approach cross-dressed men with erotic intentions (83). In most narratives on transgenders, the penetrative macho (*mayate* in Mexico, *bugarrón* in the Caribbean, *chocorrol* in Nicaragua, *michê* in Brazil, and *chongo* in Argentina) is attracted to transvestite men.

In his work on gender in the politics of daily life in Nicaragua, American ethnographer Roger N. Lancaster (1998) finds that the community judges the transvestite body as beautiful (50). This aesthetic judgment tells us of the already formed appreciation of the cross-dressing art. In Nicaragua, as in many communities of the Andes and Mesoamerica regions, transvestism has been part of traditional festivities that, as mentioned in Chapter 1, are reminiscent of the central role of transgenders in pre-Columbian cultures. Ritual cross-dressing is present in several popular festivals of the continent, such as the *tinkuy*, which Michael Horswell (2005) analyzes in Andean culture (referred to in Chapter 1), and the Xitas de Corpus (masked men of the Corpus Christi festival) in Central Mexico, in which young men trans-dress as old men and women (this also happens in the coastal areas of the Gulf of Mexico at the celebration of the end of the year). For photographer Pamela Scheinman (2013), who has worked on the Xitas de Corpus, the trans-dressed participants experience a ritual transformation to another reality (13). This is an example of the suspension of reality undertaken in the carnival. Similarly, the trans performance in the Brazilian carnival makes transgenders an object of national cultural appreciation; the carnival is an aesthetic event recognized by the community, as James N. Green (1999) highlights in his study of the centrality of the transvestite body in the national celebration (222–224).

That transgenders may be celebrated, desired, scrutinized, discriminated against, and killed reflects a contradictory field where the gender system is in crisis: that constant paradox is the queering effect of trans politics. The tension between attraction and rejection is present in most narratives of transvestites. In the most canonical transvestism novel, the aforementioned *El lugar sin límites*, this dialectic between rejection and attraction accelerates the tragedy of the sacrifice, and the book has a sad ending in which the community becomes terrified of itself for its own hatred. Pancho, a macho character, is attracted to La Manuela but has to perform hatred of her by killing her with the help of his brother-in-law. In an analysis of Catholic discourse in relation to homophobia, Gandhi Magaña Moreno (2016) concludes that killing homosexuals, and even more so transgenders, is a social mandate propelled by religious incendiary discourse (23). In various areas of Latin America, we can observe the emergence of death squads specially focused on exterminating transgenders on the streets. In 1995, for instance, a number of trans sex workers were beaten and killed in Chiapas, Mexico (Del Collado 2007: 32). In 1996, Grupo Gay da Bahía (Gay Group of Bahia) documented the existence of twelve homophobic and transphobic death squads (ICCHRLA 1996: 10).

Hyperfeminization plays a central role in the attractiveness of transvestites. *Travesti* (Transvestite) by Carlos Reyes Ávila (2009), a novel that explores the world of the trans spectacle and sex work in Torreón, Mexico, narrates the process by which Óscar, a heterosexual man, falls in love with Paulina, a trans woman, who is described as more woman than most women (25). The high level of femininity that the transgender accomplishes is a technology of the body transformation enacted as identity. The marginal space of the Zona, where prostitution is allowed, frames this transformation in the pauperized context of the excluded. This means that in the middle of the peripheral landscape, which is deemed as a risky area of the city, the construction of a fantasy based on the glamour of the divas installs a utopian fiction in the very place condemned by the "good" citizens. It is the space where the macho comes to pay for the fantasy of a constructed woman. Cuban trans sex worker Letal tells Cuban anthropologist Abel Sierra Madero (2006) that men come to her because "they are looking for a transvestite, an ambiguity between two sex, which is the most exciting option for them" (166, my translation).

Marcia Ochoa's *Queen for a Day* (2014), an ethnography of the emblematic district Avenida del Libertador in Caracas, Venezuela, reveals that transgender sex workers have occupied the very border between the rich and the poor sectors, an area reputed to be highly dangerous. Exhibiting beauty, as seen on pageant runways, is an appropriation of national symbols. This taking over of the main city's artery can be interpreted as a nationalization of the excluded body. Symbolising the border between acceptance and sacrifice, between persecution and legitimacy, and between the abject and desired, the transvestites of Avenida del Libertador describe the contradictions of the trans body in the Latin American public landscape. While it is a seductive figure that nurtures the macho's fantasies and propels an underground economic activity of sex service, it is also one of the main targets of official violence and public scorn.

Violence against the trans population has informed significant political and artistic projects that have intensified gender and sex debates since the 1980s. Besides the LGBT pride marches—which have made visible the majority of sexual diversity and provided a sense of community, which has enhanced the LGBT political presence and enhanced social acceptance—several cultural and artistic forums have constituted places of reflection and debate. In Mexico, the former Semana Cultural Gay (Gay Culture Week) (now Festival Internacional de la Diversidad Sexual, or International Festival of Sexual Diversity) has since 1987 been the most relevant forum for artists, academics, and intellectuals to reflect on issues regarding sexual diversity. In Peru, the project Museo Travesti del Perú (Peruvian Transvestites' Museum), under the direction of artist and writer Giuseppe Campuzano (2013), is a collection of images that narrate the history of the trans population in this country. This archive includes a number of newspaper articles reporting crimes against transgenders and attempts to recover the memory of a hidden history of abuses in Peruvian society. The museum is explicitly intended to empower the trans community and to enhance the recognition of sex work as an activity that produces goods and income (Campuzano 2013: 80). The museum is resignified as research that becomes action and is a community intervention where the community is not yet established: "community is a utopia, a goal" (80). By revealing the trans history of Peru, this museum project also trans-dresses the very history of the nation. The name of the choreography Campuzano presented in a dance at the launching of the book on the museum—"Toda peruanidad es un travestismo" (All about Peru Is Transvestism) (72)—suggests that transvestism is ingrained in the colonial gestures of national culture. Cross-dressing with the symbols of the other is a form of resignifying the other and finally erasing it with the harmonious discourse of brotherhood, as Jossianna Arroyo-Martínez (2003) states in her study of ethnographic discourses in Cuba and Brazil (7). In the formation of the trans archive, decolonizing the transgender has to do with recovering the queer self from that colonial erasure.

Campuzano's immediate precedent is the performance and installation group Chaclacayo, founded in 1982, whose interventions were highly controversial for their raw representations of the raped and tortured body, in reference to the hate crimes against sexual diversity by Sendero Luminoso (Shining Path) guerrillas and official armed men, and for their iconoclast versions of sacred national figures such as Santa Rosa de Lima (López 2014: 270–271). In the Museo Travesti del Perú, Campuzano departs from the Peruvian transphobia archives but also examines the daily life of the trans population, including exhibits on four jobs related to transgenders: hairdresser, sex worker, healer, and dressmaker. Despite their marginal contribution to society, trans individuals have intervened in the politics of daily life. Their very presence is a performance to be read as a challenge, as a desirable trans body is transgressive and seductive at the same time. Campuzano collects icons and objects to document the history of Peruvian transvestites but also to install the trans body within the limits of the national imaginary. The Museo Travesti del Perú is a historical exhibition, documenting the persecution, exclusion, and death of transvestites in the country. But it also celebrates the national iconography by trans-dressing the most sacred symbols of nationality, such as national saints and heroes. Javier Vargas, one of the artists included in the museum, cross-dresses the national male leaders Túpac Amaru, José Carlos Mariátegui, and José María Arguedas

(López and Campuzano 2013: 11–12). Cross-dressing national figures is an invitation to detach the binary conception of gender from the representation of the nation. Cross-dressing a father of the nation places a question mark on the gender makeup of the nation. Presenting the national father as transgender is also presenting the nation as in transit through all possible gender expressions.

The transvestite covered with national symbols has been one of the most constant visual expressions since the late 1980s. In Mexico, the Neomexicanista School, which included the most important artists of the period, had cross-dressed characters with nationalistic motifs as its main iconographic source. In painting, Julio Galán and Nahum Zenil made national dress a central element for questioning gender assumptions about national bodies. Photographs by Graciela Iturbide and Óscar Sánchez show that the trans body inhabits the quotidian space, demonstrating that transgenders are citizens that deserve recognition. This nationalizing of cross-dressing can admit at least two readings: on the one hand, it incorporates in the national discourse individuals who have long been expelled from it; on the other, the use of national symbols can be seen as a parody aiming to discredit the very basis of the nation-state. This latter interpretation is based on the iconoclast presentation of national symbols by most of these artists. The piece "Oh santa bandera" (Oh Holly Flag), by Nahum Zenil, was the center of a scandal in the 1996 Semana Cultural Gay exhibition because the artist portrayed himself with the national flag inserted in his anus. The graphic—meaning that the artist (as a metaphor for citizen) is fucked by the nation—was so direct that the authorities attempted to remove the piece from the exhibition (México 2005). Another sacrilegious queer piece famous for its effectiveness in provoking censorship is Juan Dávila's version of a transvestite Bolívar, printed on 500 postcards by the Chilean official agency Fondart, in 1994 (Long 1994). The South American independence hero was portrayed with a feminine body and making an obscene gesture with his right hand. Colombia's, Ecuador's, and Venezuela's governments sent protests to their Chilean counterpart, and the piece was finally censored. These instances of censorship demonstrate that a) national ideology is based on patriarchy, which means that treating national symbols offensively constitutes offending the heterosexist, macho hegemony; b) the sacrilegious aesthetic is an effective tool for destabilizing the gender order; and c) transvestism in contemporary art uses cross-dressing to depower political enemies (see Chapter 2), by using it to dismantle the symbolic apparatus of domination. Censorship by itself can be understood as a recognition of transgressive symbols' capacity to remove the system of beliefs and rearticulate the framework that defines the imagined community, according to how Benedict Anderson conceives of the nation. The political meaning of these sacrilegious art pieces is finally paradoxical: by using national symbols to represent queer bodies, the artistic object seems to incorporate the excluded body; but, with that very gesture, its disruption inside the patriarchal order of the nation can also take the very notion of the nation-state to the extreme by abolishing its capacity to define the collectivity. This ability informs the fear of the transvestite representation of the national.

Queer politics understood in the context of the idea of dismantling order has the effect of defining social relationships as diverse and contradictory. This is a political intervention in which queering means revealing the homophobic nature of the state and of culture in general, and orienting community politics toward a state of equal rights and wellness. In Marinella Miano Borruso's (2003) ethnography on the *muxe'* of Oaxaca, Mexico (see Chapter 1), the transgender politics concerns the community's interests, including volunteer work and preserving cultural traditions. The region's leadership in the prevention of the spread of HIV and its promotion of traditional Zapotec culture led to the selection of transgender activist Amaranta Gómez as a congressional candidate in 2006.

Argentinean historian Osvaldo Bazán (2004) describes the constant police raids against the trans population in Argentina in the 1990s. The formation of the Asociación de Travestis, Transgéneros y Transexuales de la Argentina (Argentinean Transvestites, Transgender, and Transexuals Association; ATTTA) was motivated by the official homophobia against this specific population in the nightclubs and on the streets. Police brutality provoked this organization, which later started a fight for respect and rights to the point that, in 2009, Marcela Romero, a transgender and president of the ATTTA, was promoted as a candidate for congress. Transgender leaders have succeeded in representing their communities at large, demonstrating with their leadership the incidence of queer politics.

It was also an abusive police raid against gay people gathered in the only gay bar in La Paz, Bolivia, in 1995 that marked the starting point for the formation of the Familia Galán (Galán Family), a transgender organization that has been visible in the public space in that city disputing the idea of the natural family as promoted by conservative sectors. The group's activism consists mainly of educating audiences through drag queen performances about sexual and gender diversity (Familia Galán 2012). Before its appearance in public plazas as a political transgender organization, Familia Galán members performed as *transformistas* at gay nightclub shows, where their cross-dressing goal was to reproduce a specific diva (frequently pop singers), through which they performed a subjugated, melodramatic femininity. Their coming out in the festival of sexual citizenship Placer en la Plaza (Pleasure at the Plaza), a political organization, coincided with a change in their aesthetics: now they call themselves "drag queens" (as opposed to *transformistas*), which means they are not trying to emulate any diva but to unleash their fantasy, constructing a unique character for themselves. The political presence of Familia Galán in Bolivia is so influential that one of its members,

París Galán, was elected as a member of the La Paz Legislative Assembly (*Página Siete* 2015).[2]

In the district Esperanza in the province of Trujillo, Peru, transgender leader Luisa Revilla succeeded in being elected regent in 2014. This achievement was possible thanks to the community involvement in fighting in defense of human rights and against corruption. Revilla's election as regent can be understood as a means by which citizenship has been granted to the transgendered. Revilla proudly related how she was finally elected as the candidate in her party through an internal decision, even though she had not been the favorite in the beginning (Lossio 2014–2015: 5). Ecuadorian transgender activist Diane Rodríguez was chosen as a candidate for the Constitutional Assembly in 2008 (Lavinas Picq and Viteri 2016: 1).

In the neighborhood of La Güinera in Havana, Cuba, a group of transgender spectacles has become the cultural center of the community, as presented in the documentary *Mariposas en el andamio* (Butterflies on the Scaffold) (1995), directed by Felipe Bernaza and Margarte Gipin. The political positioning of the transgender concerns the community's need to become a dynamic sector of the neighborhood. The community's particular need to be respected and recognized by the heterosexual majority sometimes takes them to the position of community leaders, as is apparent in the cases of transgender leadership previously mentioned. The emergence of transgender leadership is telling of the success in fighting homophobia in some regions of the continent, but it can also be considered a symptom of normalization. Emilio Bejel's (2001) analysis of *Mariposas en el andamio* emphasizes the very politics transvestite performance puts into effect: how it idealizes the suffering, glamorous woman stereotype and replicates patriarchal values in its exaggerated parody. It is this exaggeration

[2] I want to thank Oscar Vega Camacho, Rosario Aquim, and the organization Mujeres Creando for their views on gender and queer politics in Bolivia.

that Bejel points out as the site of transvestites' transgression; it shows gender is a construction as it denaturalizes the relationship between sex and gender (200). But cross-dressing involves a more complex process of destabilization: "these performances are symbolic attempts to break free from homophobia, from machismo and racial and class discrimination" (201). Manuela Lavinas Picq and María Amelia Viteri (2016) are aware of this normalization of the transgender when they comment on the visit of trans activist Diane Rodríguez to President Correa in Ecuador in 2013: "colonial heteronormative state formations are adjusting to contemporary sexual politics and are now engaged in the normalization of 'trans' identities and demands" (1).

If political success takes transgender into the path of normalization and integration into the heteronormative state, what then would be the political route to follow in order to escape colonization of the queer body? In his analysis of Latino/a performance in the United States, José E. Muñoz (1999) notes that queer performers try to deidentify with the stereotypical image that hegemonic apparatuses of representation, such as Hollywood, have propagated about queer bodies and race minorities (3–4). Regarding the case of Marga Gómez, a Cuban American queer performer, Muñoz points out the operation of making desirable what homophobic rules of representation have articulated as rejectable (3–5). Disidentification reorients the aesthetics of exclusion toward dearticulating the system of discrimination implemented in the dominant culture, to the point that for Muñoz queer representations constitute a counterpublic sphere. Dearticulating the heteronormative rather than integrating the queer body to the hegemonic gender system is the queer politics Muñoz proposes.

Bejel's (2001) exaggeration and Muñoz's disidentification are both deconstructive methodologies that conceive the queer approach as a form of discovering the implied politics on the cross-dressing stage. Performing cross-dressing is then a political action even in cases where politics is not intentional. In the politics of the transgender performers mentioned in these pages, we can understand the queer counterpublic sphere as a site of dispute for not only the gender system's assumptions and contentions but also the very identificatory structure that rules national identities. Thus, artist Juan Dávila's aforementioned representation of Bolívar, in Chile, and the representations of national sacred figures in the group Chaclacayo and the Museo Travesti, in Peru, impose trans iconography on central national emblematic figures, such as heroes and saints. Here disidentification consists of sharing marks of rejection with the most established sources of identity. Queering these hegemonic referents can also be read as the acknowledgment of the capacity of queerness to turn the symbolic order upside down.

On the other hand, drag queen performances implemented by Familia Galán in Bolivia, the drag group La Güinera in Cuba, and many other performers (such as the group Vecinas de la Calle J (Street J Neighbors) in Mexico) exaggerate gender attributes—that is, they distance themselves from the emulation of the feminine of traditional transvestites—to evolve toward an invention of a unique appearance. With this invention, trans-dressing becomes an event oriented toward denaturalizing gender divides and thus depowering the very system of differences that supports homophobic society.

Since the 1990s, the Theater El Hábito, today El Vicio, in Mexico City, has been the main location for queer spectacles in the country. The various performers who have presented their works in this forum have in common the use of trans-dressing, the incorporation of political theater elements in their shows, and the use of deconstructive queer positioning, not only in regard to gender and sexual subjects but also in regard to the various political and economic issues of the day. Like the popular *teatro de carpa* (tent theater), but in a middle-class setting, the shows in El Vicio bring to the public the most controversial issues of the day, making the theatrical event a place where political consensus is reached.

Some of the most memorable shows presented in this forum have featured the former owners Jesusa Rodríguez and Iliana Felipe, who cross-dressed as presidents Benito Juárez and Carlos Salinas; Tito Vasconcelos, who cross-dressed as Marta Sahagún, the first lady in the Vicente Fox government (2000–2006), famous for her corruption and pursuit of power; and Astrid Hadad's iconoclastic representation of goddesses and feminine figures of the national pantheon. The audience at El Vicio gathers around the idea of creating a consensus on a point of dissent. It is a community formed around critical pronunciations. The double politics of cabaret perturbs the public sphere with a dissent point of view—the view of a non-hetero-normed subject—and the politics implied in the body and its performance. The cross-dressed body articulating this critical enunciation is by itself a statement of having transcended gender binary assumptions. César Enríque Cabaret's "Eunucos, Castratis y Cobardis" (Eunuchs, Castrati, and Cowards) alludes to the colonial basis of Mexican masculinity, which finds a queer foundation in the macho figure. The character of the *castrato*, representing the colonial forces, subverts traditional homophobia by exposing the weakness of the macho through the imagery of castration, where emasculation is synonymous with colonization.

This universalizing of the queer, finding the queerness of the presumably non-queer, has been a constant form in which public queer interventions have been conducted. When I interviewed Nicaraguan academic and activist Camilo Antillón in June 2015, he referred to the annual event Operación Queer, in the capital city, Managua, as one in which issues of sexual diversity are debated (unpublished interview). The event's participants understand queer as a form of questioning and as freedom from fixed identities. The 2015 edition of this event had as its title the question "¿Cuál es tu coconada?," which can be translated as "What's your queerness?," a question that universalizes the possibility of being outside the hegemonic rules of body expression. This reminds us of the generalization of transvestism as a way of interpreting colonization in works by Arroyo-Martínez (2003), Campuzano (2013), and Horswell (2005). Universalizing queerness, cross-dressing hegemonic symbols, and abolishing the gender order seem to be the general lines of the utopian horizon proposed by queer interventions. Decolonizing sexuality, a concept that is heard often in academic and activist circles, is oriented toward abolishing the system of homophobia that Western gender rules have imposed on the colonized body.

Lawrence La Fountain-Stokes (2014) sees the construction of a utopia in the artistic and community work by queer artists in the Bronx neighborhood, in Manhattan, among Puerto Rican immigrants (131–132). In his review of the queer performance scene in the Puerto Rican immigrant community, he recognizes the cultural leadership queer performers have developed in the past decades. Those spaces of queer intervention—in migrant communities and indigenous towns, as well as in urban peripheries and very established middle-class settings—have in common that they are projecting a form of life that is not in place, a project for a future that is only suggested in the fantasy of attire. In the Familia Galán in Bolivia and in the Museo Travesti del Perú, the idea of trans-dressing as subjectivity under construction is prevalent. In similar terms the now extinguished drag queen group Las Vecinas de la Calle J in Mexico City conceived of its performance as the construction of a character by itself, without imitating any model (Reyes 2005).

In his discussion of Cuban writer Severo Sarduy's ideas on transvestism, Ben Sifuentes-Jáuregui (2002) underlines the notion of reflexiveness in the transvestite who *makes herself* a woman. "To define transvestism as a process of self-signification allows the possibility of autonomy and self-sufficiency to be discussed with respect to the design of subjectivity, and in some ways dislodges the figuration of transvestism from the heterosexual matrix" (Sifuentes-Jáuregui 2002: 125). According to this view, trans-dressing is a way to construct autonomy, as a self-designed subjectivity, as long as this construction dislodges heteronormative principles. The transvestism is not merely dressing like the other, as a simple inversion, as Sarduy saw it, but the possibility of abandoning hetero-normed gender expressions. José Esteban Muñoz, in the introduction to his *Cruising Utopia* (2009), locates queerness in the future, something that is not yet here but is desired and anticipated (1). The queer utopia is then a possibility for inventing one's being and hence one's history. If this self-designing of subjectivity is oriented toward a yet-to-be subject, this is a construction that happens in the quotidian world in process.

A similar view orients the concept of *transloca*, proposed by Lawrence La Fountain-Stokes (2014), which consists of a constant transformation. To be a *transloca* is to be part of the diasporic cultural process of migratory populations, to which a more complex trans experience is added: a position between the feminine and the masculine, between reason and the lack of it (2014: 141). To locate oneself in the in-between space is, on the one hand, an expression of the forceful transformation of the self when transplanted or unrooted one's their site of origin, but also, on the other hand, a form of knowledge that is intended to form with this unconformity a space for unending creation of the queer subject.

This unending creation is found in the process of sexualizing what is not conceived as a sexualized object. In this sense, queer performers have been an endless source for sexualizing the abject. In his comments about the drawings of the Peruvian artist Pedro Santillana (also known as Pedro Palanca), Javi Vargas (2014) finds that deforming the human body in this work becomes a counter-rhetoric to challenge the unidirectional hegemonic order (8). Queerness is understood, then, as unrest within the signification and the principles of sense. One of Pedro Santillana's methods for capturing his images is to furtively take photos of working-class men. This is a form of desire that consists of trespassing over the borderline between the homosexual and the heterosexual poor man

(Acuña 2014: 11). A challenge to the homophobic male, this work is a form of transgressing the macho's hermetic unreachability and to subdue him as an object of desire. The challenge of the macho is a constant topic in Latin American queer narratives; the implacable desire to seduce the expressly homophobic—the most forbidden of fruits—describes the life of the queer on the dangerous verges where homoerotic encounters happen.

It is those risky environments where the borders of heterosexuals are trespassed that for Ernesto Meccia (2011) characterize the homosexual (pre-gay) culture, which was lived with the consciousness of being on the forbidden side. Formerly, homosexuals lived in the closet and had no rights to protect them. Meccia sees this distinction in terms of two generations, the one of pre-gay homophobic times and the one of gay culture, where being out or in the closet is a determining factor. For Meccia (2011), gay culture caused the end of underground practices, making a previous way of being homosexual extinct (26). This seems to be the end of a gay utopia. But it does not mean that queer utopianism is exhausted. In contemporary critical debates, the need to decolonize Latin American culture touches gender and sexuality in the terrains of oppressive systems that have direct effect on bodies (especially those of women) and sexual diversity. Decolonizing can thus be understood as abolishing forms of homophobia that are ingrained in culture as a result of colonial patriarchal imposition. My focus in this conversation is the oppressive aspects of sexuality that are related to the newest form of colonization: the hegemony of the unregulated market, or neoliberalism, which is the subject of the next section.

Queerness and the neoliberal order

In view of the universalizing trend of queer politics, at least in its utopian articulation, the question of what is queer and what is not becomes irrelevant, as queerness is the endless possibility of estrangement of the normal (or normed). Queer designations do not necessarily depend on the activism or the market that defines cultural dominant features, but it often responds to any discourse that aims to constrain it. In the Latin American neoliberal order, being gay does not necessarily imply participation in gay activism, but it does imply a certain identification with the model propagated by the market specifically designed for gays, which is first and foremost a consumer citizenship that determines recreational activities, fashion, and ways of expressing sexuality; that defines a certain literature, film industry, and language; and that requires specific uses of space. Following the prescription of a ready-made marketable gay identity implies that sexual diversity is incorporated as a commodity and then has a merchandise value. Néstor García Canclini (1995) states that the market is used to define identities above and beyond the ties established by entities such as nation and race, around which human groups have traditionally organized:

> Men and women perceive that many of the questions asked by citizens—where do I belong and what rights does that give me, how can I inform myself, who represents my interests—can be answered more through the private consumption of goods and through mass media than by the abstract rules of democracy or by collective participation in public spaces. (29, my translation)

As an identity constituted by the market, gayness is an acculturated way of being that can be practiced all over the world and therefore can be defined by its global nature. In other words, gay culture, understood in terms of consumption, can define an identity that is globally disseminated. Nevertheless, we must emphasize that this market effect on the creation and definition of gayness takes place among middle- to upper-class Latin American homosexuals, while the other sectors, which are excluded from the market-dominated culture, end up also being excluded from the definition of the gay identity.

Mexican anthropologist Mauricio List Reyes (2005) notes that Mexico's social stratification prevents gays from "bonding in spite of shared cultural traits. And therefore we must take into account the fact that identity based on sexual preference is not given so much importance among gay Mexican individuals as to make it stand out in their social interactions" (86, my translation). List Reyes' observation forces us to turn our eyes to a population whose socioeconomic status has prevented them from affiliating with gay culture. Outside the firm terrain of gay culture, understanding sexualities requires a consideration of sexuality's intersections with cultural and political emergencies and with the legal and illegal economies.

Queerness is not so much a political movement as it is a broad range of practices and representations that expand beyond the proposals gay culture makes about identity. If globalization has had any consequences in the area of culture, it has been to diversify the sources of signs such that queer culture cannot be defined only by what is produced and propagated from the rich Western countries but must also include meanings circulated in networks of global contact. It is in this contact—which happens in the various types of displacements, from tourism to migrations and from slavery to exile— that inequalities and forms of oppression deepen; however, a great diversity of body expressions have also emerged as result of cultural and political effervescence. As Arnoldo Cruz-Malavé and Martin F. Manalanzan (2002) propose in the introduction to their *Queer Globalizations*, the globalization of capital has opened up routes for "cross-cultural engagements that are more respectful of queer cultures and lives" (4). Indeed, a broad margin of liberating zones for queer expressions is in place; however, the intensification of forms of gender and sexual violence and the commodification of the body raise serious questions and challenges for all body-related studies.

While global markets have created exchange networks that decenter queer cultural practices, other networks devalue and colonize subaltern bodies through slave markets, pederasty, and child pornography—ethical issues that must be addressed urgently. The contradictions and diverse forms of power that accompany globalization and that are described by Ianni (1999) and by Hardt and Negri (2000), among others, are particularly crucial in the area of queerness. The market, long an apparatus that legitimizes and merges social practices, has also become a mechanism for violating the human rights of children, who, as in the cases that the journalist Lydia Cacho denounced in her book *Los demonios del Edén* (*The Devils of Eden*) (2006), are not protected at all by the Mexican justice system (53–73). If the global order gives preferential treatment to that which can enter the circuit of the global market, then the prostitution of poor children and adolescents for the purposes of international tourism in Acapulco, Cancún, and many places in the Caribbean, in as much as it produces capital, is immune from the law. The businesses of prostitution and child pornography survive thanks to the fact that an increasing population has created a demand. This form of consumerism cannot be related in any way to the behaviors of gayness—in the liberating sense, at least. These behaviors are a symptom of life "in the closet," of the furtive behavior that homophobic society enforces. Thus we can affirm that it is not only the positive aspects of the gay liberation movement that have arrived from the north; Latin America is now also experiencing the effects of a homophobia that finds its escape valve in the exploitation of those who are the most vulnerable.

The Mexican American sociologist Lionel Catnú (2002) proposes that we should "move away from one-dimensional cultural models and examine these sexualities from a more complex and materialist perspective that recognizes that culture, social relations, and identities are embedded in global processes" (140). For him, sex tourism, intensified since the 1990s, constitutes a new form of colonialism that is necessarily transforming sex culture. Queer tourism is attracted to an exotic product that promises a rare sexual–cultural experience. I understand cultural experience as the consumption of otherness conceived as value in terms of sex and ethnicity, following Jacqueline Sánchez Taylor's (2000) suggestion in her work on sexual tourism in the Caribbean (42). The macho or Latin lover's sexuality as portrayed in the colonialist archives, which assign primitiveness and some natural force to the perceived premodern bodies, is resignified in the neoliberal version of colonialism as a commodity. If, according to Dennis Altman (2001), gay and lesbian culture has been one of the most globalized subcultures to the point that people affiliated with this identity have more in common with others around the world than they have in common with their own societies (86–87), we can then say that gay globalized culture subsumes poor locals from the premodern, pre-gay, macho sexuality and then performs a colonialist cultural practice. The relationship between tourist and sex worker expropriates the traditional macho homoeroticism in which the macho, who plays the dominant role in homoerotic sexual contact, is not considered a homosexual. This form of bisexual practice has been amply studied as one of the most distinctive aspects of Mediterranean— then Latino—masculine sexuality (see Garber 2000; Decenas 2011; Domínguez Ruvalcaba 2007; Prieur 1998). Globalization not only homogenizes cultures but also redefines the roles of cultures in a new, unequal distribution of material and symbolic goods. Globalized gays consume the premodern expression of a perceived premodern, nonglobalized culture.

These "pre-modern sexualities" are imagined from a metropolitan gay perspective that misrepresents non-gay homoeroticism as *machista* and homophobic. This perception understands that metropolitan Western sexual categories are more liberating than those of the postcolonial countries. The argument that, before gay culture arrived, a nonhomophobic homoerotic practice (that is to say, separate from the homophobic tradition of Western heterosexual hegemony) already existed in Mexico can be inferred from the ethnographic work of Guillermo Núñez Noriega (1999) with respect to the sexuality of men from Sonora, Mexico. Núñez reports that a large portion of those he interviewed about their relationships with other men refused to identify themselves as gays, *jotos*, *mayates*, homosexuals, or bisexuals. They preferred to define themselves simply as men who like *el cotorreo* (to mess around or have a good time). This term places "the homoerotic practice in the field of adventure, fun, and shared pranks and jokes" (Núñez Noriega 2001: 27, my translation); in this way, categories of identity that normalize sexuality can be avoided, and eroticism is practiced within the realm of friendship (homosociety) and does not connote romantic love or partnership. According to Núñez Noriega, the politics of identity (into which the gay movement inscribes itself) imposed by the patriarchal structure (understood as the homophobic and misogynist hierarchy) is subverted by this lack of definition. Just as is the case with the character Adonis in *El vampiro de la Colonia Roma*, by Mexican writer Luis Zapata (2009) (see Chapter 3), we can see a major asymmetry between the concept of gayness as identity and the practices of homoeroticism in the context of tourism.

It is appropriate to question whether, through their "liberated" practices, the men from Sonora are able to escape the homophobia endemic to Mexican society. It would be possible to say that their reluctance to define or name homoerotic contact stems precisely from homophobia. After all, a large number of these men are heads of families and live publicly as heterosexuals, a fact that is in no way nebulous or unnamed. Then, what at first appears to be a liberating utopia is on the contrary a strategy by which hegemonic heterosexuality aims to maintain its place as the only legitimate and normalized form of sexuality. In his most well-known book, *Sexo entre varones* (Sex between Males) (1999; first published in 1994), Nuñez Noriega affirms that achieving "homosexual identity depends, in large part, on the structure of the sexual field, and on the fight to achieve legitimate representation of sexual existence" (167). With this statement, Núñez Noriega implicitly recognizes that the undeclared homosexuality of his interviewees cannot be legitimized because it is not represented. Perhaps what is missing from the proposal of nondefinition (as a liberating practice) is the political aspect: if nondefinition is aimed at delegitimizing heterosexual structures, then a truly liberating act has been achieved; however, if not, we are only observing another of many forms of homophobia that keep homoerotic practices at risk and in the shadows. Not defining homoerotic sex as homosexual, but only as a recreational practice without implications in the realm of subjectivity, denies the possibility that homoerotic practice plays a role in articulating any political discourse about the colonizing effects of sex tourism.

The possibility of taking over the public sphere with artistic, intellectual, and political interventions has been constant throughout the history of sexual diversity on the continent. From the LGBT movement to the drag queens' aesthetic revolution, queer politics has been a process of inclusion in citizenship based on differences in sexuality and gender expressions. These self-determined movements have reconfigured the frames of citizenship in many countries of the region. As a result, queer politics, or the politics of sexual, affective, and body diversity, has played a determining role in the changes that have been made in the paradigms that inform rules, policies, and discourses. In earlier chapters, I have focused on projects to queer gender and sexuality (and then institutions and identities) and projects to construct citizenship for those sectors largely excluded and victimized because of their gender or sexuality.

But what can be said regarding those sexualities that are not freely practiced? How can sex slavery and sex service forced by economic and social conditions be understood from a queer studies approach? The first question has to do with the use up to now of queer studies to orient a liberation project based on the incorporation of queer bodies into a citizenry. This movement has consisted of a process of converting the excluded or the abject into a desirable body, as Jacobo Schifter (1999) interprets the process of cross-dressing in his ethnography on Costa Rican transgenders (27). The ultimate objective of this liberation perspective is acceptance and integration. Let us understand this integration as a form of signifying and practicing the body that is in tandem with the norms of desire that rule the market order. This means that to be integrated into the neoliberal order is to be governed by the rules of consumption that ultimately define it. But the consumed bodies, the ones who are not free to be consumers in this market game, seem to be out of ideas when it comes to queer liberation. This is perhaps one of the most concerning issues of present times in light of the lack of self-determination in disadvantaged populations in Latin America. The increasing information that is being leaked into the media, especially social media, regarding child pornography, human trafficking, sex slavery, and sex tourism demands our attention.

In the cases of slavery and sex service, the desire to abuse, to humiliate, and to trade with others' bodies prevails over the victim's desire. It is the privilege of buying the enjoyment of another's body that makes the consumer tourist a colonizer, an expropriator of the poor's body. Suspension of one's desire (often suspension of one's gender identity) to perform what the other expects is the central theme in my work on the figure of the *mayate* in my book *Modernity and the Nation in Mexican Representations of Masculinity* (Domínguez Ruvalcaba 2007: 131–147). In this work I argue that men who perform the dominant role in homoerotic encounters but identify themselves as heterosexuals are the queerest form of masculinity in Mexican sexual culture. *Mayate* is a pre-gay category that persists on the margins of gay culture, which I insist on calling hegemonic because of its central, legitimizing position. *Mayate* is another name for the active member in the traditional homoerotic relationship, where the *joto* is the passive homosexual. The *mayate* does not identify himself as homosexual and therefore cannot be defined as gay. He has sexual relations with women and justifies his sexual relations with *jotos* by asking them for favors or money in exchange for sex. The *mayate* is, then, a sort of fortuitous prostitute. It is from this angle that the *mayate* maintains contact with gay culture, and from there access to gay tourism. Ethnographies by Joseph Carrier (2002) and Annick Prieur (1998), the most canonical works on homosexuality in Mexico, dedicate several pages to this figure. But the documentary video *Amor chacal* (Chacal Love) (2001), by Juan Carlos Bautista and Victor Jaramillo, is particularly valuable for pointing to the status of the *mayate* in the globalized society. Here, we can observe how the *mayate* is redefined within the frame of contemporary gay culture. The documentary functions as the travelogue of a gay couple on the Veracruz coast. Repeatedly the *mayate* is presented as a tourist attraction of which the whole coastal society is aware. The locals justify the *mayate*'s activities as a traditional practice. Just like the *muxe'* in Oaxaca, the *mayate* are traditional homoerotic subjects who take on the value of ethnographic objects redefined by the tourist market. In this way, the *mayate*, like the *muxe'*, is part of the catalog of symbols and traditional practices of pre-gay culture for the global market of cultural experiences.

Nevertheless, we cannot consider the *muxe'* and the *mayate* to be figures who rescue Mexico from the globalization of gay culture, as their value as ethnographic subjects and tourist products makes them part of flow of signs that globalization has put into motion.

Far from being expressions of resistance to gay culture, they serve as others, nurturing the colonizing fantasies of global gays. Yet we cannot declare this otherness without also recognizing that these subaltern forms of sexuality have achieved their legitimacy in relation to their respective local settings, thanks in part to the attention paid to them by the gay community. This process of legitimization brings us back to queer theory's criticism of the politics of identity.

In his ethnography on male prostitution in Brazil, *O negócio do Michê: A prostituição viril* (The Business of the Michê: The Masculine Prostitute) (1987), Argentinean writer and anthropologist Néstor Perlongher details the economy and social structure of male prostitution in São Paulo. This seminal work outlined how prostitution work constructs a sexual identity by itself, although this is mediated by the inequality that is endemic to Latin America. The *mayate*, *mîche*, or *chongo* has been a poor, often dark-skinned sexual provider for homosexuals since long before the neoliberal era. The gesture in which such men deny that they experience attraction to the homosexual men who pay for their sex service is referred to in the travel magazines Lionel Cantú (2002) quotes as a butch expression charged of hypermasculinity. It is hard to determine whether the *mayate*'s sexuality is chosen freely or coerced by others. It is a problematic identity that finally becomes recodified in the context of the contemporary sex market circuit that the touristic industry enhances. If we consider that the male prostitute practices homoeroticism as a form of survival (similarly to how the figure of the *jinetero/a*, the male or female prostitute for tourists in Cuba, is constructed), then we are talking of prostitution as a last resort for the marginalized. Let us say that there are various levels of coerciveness: in the case of *jineteros* and other sex workers, there is a socioeconomic emergency that forces participation in an economic activity consisting of renting the body. This is a structurally created market that is implicitly legitimized by society. But there is another level of forced sex, which formed a part of the history of Latin American slavery: the abduction of European girls to be forced to prostitution in Buenos Aires in the 1800s, as described by Donna Guy in her *Sex and Danger in Buenos Aires: Prostitution, Family and Nation in Argentina* (1991), can be seen as a precedent for contemporary webs of sex slavery denounced by Argentinean activist Susana Trimarco (Fundación María de los Ángeles n.d.). Works by journalists such as Lydia Cacho (2006) and Sanjuana Martínez (2009) have unveiled powerful webs of pederasts who abuse children through a globally established system of child prostitution and through the child pornography industry. At this point, the difference between homosexuality and heterosexuality is irrelevant and the issue of the liberation of sexuality is out of the question. These bodies are not bodies for themselves but for others, as their sexuality is expropriated forcefully or for their survival; thus, their signification as homosexual, pederastic, gerontophilic, fetishistic, etc. can be only understood as coercive sexuality—sexuality constructed by and for the consumer.

The consumer performs his/her desire and the provider learns a sexuality that consists of serving the consumer's whims: that is, a sexuality normalized by the market rules. The sexualities produced in this system of body consumption are designed violently. The acceleration of the sexual market has consolidated a system of victimization as a type of flourishing, transnational economy. This market depends on a system of power constructed for the purpose of violating the law, prominently laws concerning human rights. This perverted system positions itself as supremacist as it breaks the norm that protects the integrity of bodies. It is a practice of domination that consists of extracting from the objectified person all of his/her value as merchandise in the context of sexual abuse, or the sexual abuse as merchandise by itself.

The system that commodifies bodies produces, then, an oppressive technology where sex is coerced and where any practice that can otherwise define sexual identities is here practiced for coercion, suppressing the subject in favor of the illegal market of forced sex. In talking about sexual exploitation, the focus is not to liberate the subject to enable him/her to practice a dissident sexuality but rather to liberate the subject from the oppression through and for exploitative sex. This is not liberation from sexuality (the subjectivity produced through sex) but from the expropriation of it for the enjoyment of sex consumers— those who possesses the privilege of consuming disempowered individuals.

The divide between those who have the privilege of enjoyment and those who offer the service of being abused defines a form of economy that continues the dominant practices of war, enslavement, and colonization. In the context of this panorama of the expropriation of sexuality from the subject, the capacity of making decisions about our own bodies has become the main objective in the proposal of a politics that responds to the oppressive system, to the contemporary colonizer, and to the exploiter of pleasurable resources.

Conclusion

The two aspects of queerness focused on in this chapter are not the only challenges queer studies is facing at present in Latin America. Issues of intersexuality, which interrogates the heteronormative constraints of the binary order of differentiation, have also been relevant in recent years; in addition, studies of disabilities and body transformation have become a rich area for considering subjectivities and bodies beyond the sexuality episteme. New issues that are pervading the gay and sexuality fields are, according to my reading of the emerging scholarship, activism, art, and the route that queer studies and interventions seem to follow in Latin America. This development means that two of the main agendas the queer perspective has to address are the invention of a subjectivity free from ready-made social categories (like the politics of drag queens proposes) and the decolonization of bodies expropriated for the sex market in the contemporary neoliberal system.

Conclusion

Latin American discussions on queer issues disseminated in academic works, films, artistic interventions, and body politics constitute a rampant field of knowledge and action that is reconfiguring and increasing its presence in social life. This book is just an invitation to continue this conversation. The review I proposed is the route of a personal itinerary in Latin American sexuality studies; it is part of an intellectual adventure consisting of crossing restlessly between north and south, bringing every time a different set of questions to be considered. Here I summarize how these themes—the main issues found in the conversations of this academic field since the 1990s—have been addressed in this book.

First, colonial queerness opens the way to understanding coloniality as a form of reduction of the multiplicity to a binary heterosexual gender. In this sense, translating Western culture into the native cultures of South America consists of erasing and proscribing diverse sexual practices. The history of pre-Columbian and colonial sexualities scrutinizes the criminal archive, confessionary manuals, rituals, and magic texts to find traces of proscribed queerness, creating an archeology of the untold history of forbidden sexualities.

Second, modernity installed the notion of the secular nation and the concept of the science of medicine and criminology by which bodies are controlled, punished, secluded, and expelled from communities. Homophobic nationalistic discourses use queer representations such as transvestism to attack political enemies and criticize antinational attitudes, disqualifying queerness in terms of pro-colonialism, imperialism, and betrayal. Despite this nationalistic hostility toward sexual difference in most of modern Latin American history, in literature and the arts the basis of a queer politics has emerged as an antihomophobic response to conservative intolerance. Queerness can be seen as the disturbing side of modernity. Inside the closet, several members of the lettered city, the intellectual elite, started a process of queering the nation in their aesthetic and critical projects. This queering can also be understood as a form of depatriarchalizing the state, but it still does not embody an explicitly political proposal.

Third, LGBT politics is closely related to Marxist–Leninist political discourses and has articulated a revolutionary queer program, despite the reluctance of leftist groups to incorporate a dissident sexual agenda. The AIDS pandemic restructured the movement with a new discourse of rights instead of the liberation agenda of the 1970s. The LGBT movement has since then been a political force that has achieved several demands in the major countries in the region. Gay culture, on the other hand, has established a divide between the middle-class, cosmopolitan gay culture and the traditional oppressive and homophobic sexualities, revealing economic and political intersections with sex, race, and class.

Fourth, trans politics emerged from the victimizing, endemic transphobia in Latin America. From the difficulties of their struggles, in several instances trans activists came to be community leaders. In this transformation, the trans construction evolved from being a diva-melodramatic imitation to a nonimitative invention of herself that articulates a queer utopia.

Fifth, one of the biggest challenges in the field of sexuality is the issue of coercive and forced sexuality. The development of a sex market based on slavery and prostitution entered into for survival raises several questions about consumption and disposability in the sexual economy of the neoliberal system. Ethical and political reflections on sex abuse and sex crimes are pushing gender, sexuality, and queer studies to the side so that this emergency can be addressed.

A still wider number of works on body difference politics need to be considered. Disability studies, body transformation technologies, posthuman perspectives on sexuality, and fat studies are topics on the body that are finding their way into contemporary conversations and that deserve scholars' attention in future projects.

References

Acuña, Héctor. (2014). "Palanca o el hiperrealismo perverso de un fetichista consumado." *Crónicas de la diversidad* (August–September), 10–11.

Ahmadov, Anar, and Farid Guliyev. (2016). *Tackling the Resource Curse: The Role of Democracy in Achieving Sustainable Development in Resource-Rich Countries.* Stockholm: International IDEA.

Altman, Dennis. (2001). *Global Sex.* Chicago: University of Chicago Press.

Alvarez, Sonia E. (2014). "Introduction." In Sonia E. Alvarez, Claudia de Lima Costa, Verónica Feliu, Rebecca Hester, Norma Klahn, and Millie Thayer, eds. *Translocalities/Translocalidades: Feminist Politics of Translation in Latin/a Américas.* Durham, NC: Duke University Press, 7–26.

Anzaldúa, Gloria. (1999). *Borderlands/La Frontera: The New Mestiza.* San Francisco: Aunt Lute Books.

— (2002a). "Now Let Us Shift … the Path of Conocimiento … Inner Work, Public Acts." In Gloria Anzaldúa and Analouise Keating, eds. *This Bridge We Call Home.* New York: Routledge, 540–578.

— (2002b). "(Un)natural Bridges, (Un)safe Spaces." In Gloria Anzaldúa and Analouise Keating, eds. *This Bridge We Call Home.* New York: Routledge, 1–5.

— (2015). "La Prieta." In Cherríe Moraga and Gloria Anzaldúa, eds. *This Bridge Called my Back: Writings by Radical Women of Color.* New York: SUNY Press, 198–209.

Arroyo-Martínez, Jossianna. (2003). *Travestismos culturales: Literatura y etnografía en Cuba y Brasil.* Pittsburgh: Instituto de Literatura Iberoamericana.

Aznares, Juan Jesús. (2013). "Nicolás Maduro y la homofobia en América Latina." *El País*, March 18. Downloaded December 1, 2015. http://elpais.com/elpais/2013/03/19/opinion/1363704621_194415.html.

Balderston, Daniel. (1998). "Poetry, Revolution, Homophobia: Polemics from the Mexiacan Revolution." In Sylvia Molloy and Robert McKee, eds. *Hispanisms and Homosexualities*. Durham: Duke University, 57–75.

— (2000). *Borges: Realidades y simulacros*. Buenos Aires: Biblos.

Bazán, Osvaldo. (2004). *Historia de la homosexualidad en Argentina: De la conquista de América al siglo XXI*. Buenos Aires: Marea.

Bejel, Emilio. (2001). *Gay Cuban Nation*. Chicago: University of Chicago Press.

Bhabha, Homi. (1994). *The Location of Culture*. New York: Routledge.

Bilbao, Bárbara Soledad. (2012). "Frente de liberación homosexual (1971–1976): prácticas comunicacionales de resistencia y resignificaciones en la historia reciente." *Question*, 1:33, 23–32.

Buarque de Holanda, Sérgio. (1936). *Raízes do Brazil*. Rio de Janeiro: J. Olympio.

Buffington, Robert. (2003). "Homophobia and the Mexican Working Class, 1900–1910." In Robert M. Irwin, Edward J. McCaughan, and Michelle Rocío Nasser, eds. *The Famous 41: Sexuality and Social Control in Mexico, c.1901*. New York: Palgrave Macmillan, 193–225.

Cacho, Lydia. (2006). *Los demonios del Edén*. Mexico: Grijalbo.

Campuzano, Giuseppe. (2013). *Saturday Night Thriller y otros escritos, 1998–2013*. Lima: Estruendomudo.

Cano, Gabriela. (1999). "La íntima felicidad del coronel Robles." *Equis, Cultura y Sociedad*, 14, 25–35.

Cantú, Lionel. (2002). "De Ambiente: Queer Tourism and the Shifting Boundaries of the Mexican Male Sexualities." *GLQ: A Journal of Lesbian and Gay Studies*, 8:1–2, 139–166.

Careaga, Gloria. (2005). "Los acuerdos internacionales: Un reto pendiente de la política nacional." In Edith Yesenia Peña Sánchez, Francisco Ortiz Pedraza, and Lilia Hernádez Albarrán, eds. *Memorias de la II semana cultural de la diversidad sexual*. Mexico: Instituto Nacional de Antropología e Historia, 305–311.

Carrier, Joseph. (2002). *De los otros: Intimidad y homosexualidad entre los hombres del occidente y el noroeste de México*. Mexico: Editorial Pandora.

Carrillo, Héctor. (2002). *The Night Is Young: Sexuality in Mexico in the Time of AIDS*. Chicago: University of Chicago Press.

Castañeda, Jorge G. (1993). *La utopía desarmada*. Mexico: Joaquín Mortiz.

Chávez-Silverman, Susana, and Librada Hernández, eds. (2000). *Reading and Writing the Ambiente: Queer Sexualities in Latino, Latin American, and Spanish Culture*. Madison: University of Wisconsin Press.

Cohen, Jeffrey Jerome. (1996). *Monster Theory*. Minneapolis: University of Minnesota Press.

Cornejo Polar, Antonio. (2003 [1994]). *Escribir en el aire: Ensayo sobre la heterogeneidad sociocultural en las literaturas andinas*. Lima: Centro de Estudios Literarios Antonio Cornejo Polar.

Cornell, Drucilla. (2004). "Gender in America." In Nadia Tazi, ed. *Keywords. Gender*. New York: Other Press, 33–54.

Cruikshank, Margaret. (1992). *The Gay and Lesbian Liberation Movement*. New York: Routledge.

Cruz-Malavé, Arnoldo, and Martin F. Manalansan. (2002). "Introduction." In Arnoldo Cruz-Malavé and Martin F. Manalansan, eds. *Queer Globalizations*. New York: New York University Press.

Cuba, Lucero. (2012). *Entre orgullos y resistencias. Una aproximación al movimiento LGBT en Perú*. Lima: Programa Democracia y Transformación Social.

Cutter, Martha J. (2005). *Lost & Found in Translation*. Chapel Hill: University of North Carolina Press.

De la Cuadra, Fernando. (2015). "Indigenous people, socio-environmental conflict and post-development in Latin America." *Ambiente & Sociedade*, 18:2, 23–40.

De la Dehesa, Rafael. (2010). *Queering the Public Sphere in Mexico and Brazil: Sexual Rights Movements in Emerging Democracies*. Durham: Duke University Press.

Decenas, Carlos U. (2011). *Tacit Subjects: Belonging and Same-Sex Desire among Dominican Immigrant Men*. Durham: Duke University Press.

Del Collado, Fernando. (2007). *Homofobia: Odio, crimen y justicia*. Mexico: Tusquets.

Dhawan, Nikita. (2016). "Homonationalism and state-phobia: The postcolonial predicament of queering modernities." In María Amelia Viteri and Manuela Lavinas Picq, eds. *Queering Paradigms V: Queering Narratives of Modernity*. Oxford: Peter Lang, 51–68.

Díaz Arciniegas, Víctor. (1989). *Querella por la cultura "revolucionaria" (1925)*. Mexico: Fondo de Cultura Económica.

Díez, Jordi. (2010). "The Importance of Policy Frames in Contentious Politics: Mexico's National Antihomophobia Campaign." *Latin American Research Review*, 45:1, 33–54.

— (2015). *The Politics of Gay Marriage in Latin America: Argentina, Chile, and Mexico.* New York: Cambridge University Press.

Domínguez Ruvalcaba, Héctor. (2007). *Modernity and the Nation in Mexican Representations of Masculinity: From Sensuality to Bloodshed.* New York: Palgrave.

Donoso, José. (1966). *El lugar sin límites.* Mexico: Joaquín Mortiz.

Ellis, Robert Richmond. (2000). "Introduction." In Susana Chávez-Silverman and Librada Hernández, eds. *Reading and Writing the Ambiente: Queer Sexualities in Latino, Latin American, and Spanish Culture.* Madison: University of Wisconsin Press, 3–18.

Epps, Brad. (2008). "Retos, riesgos, pautas y promesas de la teoría *queer.*" *Revista Iberoamericana,* 74:225, 897–920.

Estrada Corona, Adrián. (2010). "El proceso de lucha del colectivo lésbico-gay: Entrevista con Alejandro Brito." *Revista Digitas Universitaria,* 11:9. Downloaded July 28, 2015. http://www.revista.unam.mx/vol.11/num9/art91.

Falconí Trávez, Diego. (2016). "Hansel/Hedwig, la Casa Playo, la Tunda: Transculturaciones y decolonialidades literarias *queer,* cuir, cuy(r) en América Latina." In María Amelia Viteri and Manuela Lavinas Picq, eds. *Queering Paradigms V: Queering Narratives of Modernity.* Oxford: Peter Lang, 395–316.

Familia Galán. (2012). "La apropiación de espacios públicos desde el transformismo." In David Aruquipa Pérez, Paula Estenssoro Velaochaga, and Pablo Céspedes Vargas, eds. *Memorias colectivas: Miradas a la Historia del Movimiento TLGB de Bolivia.* La Paz: Conexión, 239–241.

Fernández, Josefina. (2005). "Travestismo y violencia policial: De cada cien de nosotras, 85 hemos padecido algún tipo de violencia policial." In Lohana Berkins and Josefina Fenández, eds. *La gesta del nombre propio: Informe sobre la situación de la comunidad travesti en la Argentina.* Buenos Aires: Ediciones Madres de Plaza de Mayo, 39–65.

Figari, Carlos. (2014). "Fagotizando lo queer en el Cono Sur." In Diego Falconí Trávez, Santiago Castellanos, and María Amelia Viteri, eds. *Resentir lo queer en América Latina: Diálogos desde/con el sur.* Barcelona: Egales, 63–79.

Fiol-Matta, Licia. (2002). *A Queer Mother for the Nation: The State and Gabriela Mistral.* Minneapolis: University of Minnesota Press.

Foster, David. (2000). "Evita Perón, Juan José Sebreli, and Gender." In Susana Chávez-Silverman and Librada Hernández, eds. *Reading and Writing the Ambiente: Queer Sexualities in Latino, Latin American, and Spanish Culture*. Madison: University of Wisconsin Press, 218–238.

Foucault, Michel. (1980). "The confession of the flesh [interview, 1977]." In Colin Gordon, ed. *Power/Knowledge: Selected Interviews and Other Writings*, New York: Pantheon Books, 194–228.

— (1990 [1976]). *The History of Sexuality*. Trans. Robert Hurley. New York: Vintage Books.

— (2006 [1961]). *History of Madness*. Trans. Jonathan Murphy and Jean Khalfa. London: Routledge.

Frente de Liberación Homosexual. (2011). "Sexo y Revolución." *Taringa*, June 1. Downloaded July 28, 2015. http://www.taringa.net/comunidades/orgullolgbt/1588684/Frente-de-Liberacion-Homosexual-Sexo-y-Revolucion.html.

Fundación María de los Ángeles. (n.d.). "Susana Trimarco." Downloaded December 1, 2015. http://www.fundacionmariadelosangeles.org/susana-trimarco.htm.

Garber, Marjorie. (2000). *Bisexuality & the Eroticism of Everyday Life*. New York: Routledge.

García Canclini, Néstor. (1995). *Consumidores y ciudadanos: Conflictos multiculturales de la globalización*. Mexico: Grijalbo.

Gargallo, Francesca. (2014). *Feminismos desde Abya Yala: Ideas y Proposiciones de las mujeres de 607 pueblos de nuestra América*. Mexico: Corte y Confección.

Garza Carvajal, Federico. (2003). *Butterflies Will Burn: Prosecuting Sodomites in Early Modern Spain and Mexico*. Austin: University of Texas Press.

Geneva Declaration on Armed Violence and Development. (2015). "Global burden of armed violence 2015." Downloaded July 21, 2016. http://www.genevadeclaration.org/measurability/global-burden-of-armed-violence/gbav-2015/chapter-3.html.

González Casanova, Pablo (1969). *Sociología de la explotación*. Mexico: Siglo XXI.

González Pérez, César O. (2003). *Travestidos al desnudo: Homosexualidad, identidades y luchas territoriales en Colima*. Mexico: Miguel Ángel Porrúa-CIESAS.

Gramsci, Antonio. (1971). *Selections from the Prison Notebooks*, edited by Quintin Hoare and Goeffrey Nowell Smith. New York: International Publishers.

Green, James N. (1999). *Beyond Carnival: Male Homosexuality in Twentieth-Century Brazil*. Chicago: University of Chicago Press.

Grupo Gay da Bahia. (2015). "Assassinato de Homossexuais (LGBT) no Brasil: Relatório 2014." Downloaded September 1, 2015. https://

homofobiamata.files.wordpress.com/2015/01/relatc3b3rio-2014s. pdf.

Gutiérrez, Laura G. (2010). *Performing Mexicanidad: Vendidas y Cabareteras on the Transnational Stage*. Austin: University of Texas Press.

Guy, Donna. (1991). *Sex and Danger in Buenos Aires: Prostitution, Family and Nation in Argentina*. Lincoln: University of Nebraska Press.

Guzmán, Manolo. (1997). "'Pa la Escuelita con mucho cuidao y por la orillita': A Journey through the Contested Terrains of the Nation and Sexual Orientation." In Frances Negrón Muntaner and Ramón Grosfoguel, eds. *Puerto Rican Jam: Rethinking Colonialism and Nationalism*. Minneapolis: University of Minnesota Press, 209–228.

Hardt, Michael, and Antonio Negri. (2000). *Empire*. Cambridge: Harvard University Press.

Hawley, John, ed. (2001). *Postcolonial, Queer: Theoretical Intersections*. Albany: State University of New York Press, 2001.

Hernández, Wilfredo. (2006). "Medicina, homosexualidad y política en Cuba finisecular: La polémica de los dependientes españoles de comercio." *Revista de Estudios Hispánicos*, 40:1, 25–48.

Hernández Cabrera, Porfiro Miguel. (2005). "El movimiento lésbico, gay, bisexual y transgenérico y la construcción social de la identidad gay en la Ciudad de México." In Edith Yesenia Peña Sánchez, Francisco Ortiz Pedraza, and Lilia Hernádez Albarrán, eds. *Memorias de la II semana cultural de la diversidad sexual*. Mexico: Instituto Nacional de Antropología e Historia, 287–304.

Horan, Elizabeth Rosa. (2000). "Alternative Identities of Gabriel(a) Mistral 1906–1920." In Susana Chávez-Silverman and Librada Hernández, ed. *Reading and Writing the Ambiente: Queer Sexualities in Latino, Latin American, and Spanish Culture*. Madison: University of Wisconsin Press, 147–177.

Horswell, Michael J. (2005). *Decolonizing the Sodomite: Queer Tropes of Sexuality in Colonial Andean Culture*. Austin: University of Texas Press.

Ianni, Octavio. (1999). *Desafios da globalização*. Petrópolis: Editora Vozes.

ICCHRLA (Inter-Church Committee of Human Rights in Latin America). (1996). *La violencia al descubierto: Represión contra las lebianas y homosexuales en América Latina*. Toronto: ICCHRLA. Downloaded December 1, 2015. http://www.choike.org/documentos/gays_violencia.pdf.

Irwin, Robert M. (2000). "As Invisible as He Is: The Queer Enigma of Xavier Villaurrutia." In Susana Chávez-Silverman and Librada Hernández, eds. *Reading and Writing the Ambiente: Queer Sexualities in Latino, Latin American, and Spanish Culture*. Wisconsin: University of Wisconsin Press, 114–146.

Irwin, Robert M., Edward J. McCaughan, and Michelle Rocío Nasser, eds. (2003). *The Famous 41: Sexuality and Social Control in Mexico, 1901*. New York: Palgrave Macmillan.

Jagose, Annmarie. (1996). *Queer Theory: An Introduction*. New York: New York University Press.

Jones, Daniel. (2008). "Estigmatización y discriminación a adolescentes varones homosexuales." In Mario Pecheny, Carlos Figary, and Daniel Jones, eds. *Todo sexo es político: Estudios sobre sexualidades en Argentina*. Buenos Aires: Libros del Zorzal, 47–72.

Keating, Analouise. (1998). "(De)centering the Margins? Identity Politics and Tactical (Re)naming." In Sandra Kumamoto Stanley, ed. *Other Sisterhoods: Literary Theory and US Women of Color*. Urbana: University of Illinois Press, 23–43.

King, Rosamond S. (2014). *Island Bodies: Transgressive Sexualities in the Caribbean Imagination*. Gainesville: University Press of Florida.

La Fountain-Stokes, Lawrence. (2009). *Queer Rican: Cultures and Sexualities in the Diaspora*. Minneapolis: University of Minnesota Press.

— (2014). "Epistemología de la loca: Localizando a la transloca en la transdiáspora." In Diego Falconí Trávez, Santiago Castellanos, and María Amelia Viteri, eds. *Resentir lo queer en América Latina: Diálogos desde/con el sur*. Barcelona: Egales, 133–146.

Lancaster, Roger N. (1998). "La actuación de Guto: Notas sobre el travestismo en la vida cotidiana." In Daniel Balderston and Donna J. Guy, eds. *Sexo y sexualidades en América Latina*. Buenos Aires: Paidós, 29–68.

Lara y Mateos, Rosa María. (2006). *Vivir muriendo: La estigmatización a hombres que tienen sexo con hombres (HSH) seropositivos del puerto de Veracruz*. Mexico: CENSIDA, Colectivo Sol.

Lavinas Picq, Manuela, and María Amelia Viteri. (2016). "Introducciones: Trastocar Narratives of Modernity." In María Amelia Viteri and Manuela Lavinas Picq, eds. *Queering Paradigms V: Queering Narratives of Modernity*. Oxford: Peter Lang, 1–18.

Lemebel, Pedro. (1997 [1995]). *La esquina es mi corazón: Crónica urbana*. Santiago: Cuarto Propio.

— (2000 [1996]). *Loco afán*. Barcelona: Anagrama.

— (2001). *Tengo miedo torero*. Santiago: Planeta.

— (2013). "La insaciable sed metafórica [interview with Héctor Domínguez Ruvalcaba in 2001]." *La Gaceta de la Universidad de Guadalajara*, October 14, 6–7.

Letra Ese. (2015). "Informe crímene de odio por homofobia." Downloaded October 21, 2015. http://www.letraese.org.mx/proyectos/proyecto-1-2.

Lezama Lima, José. (1977). *Oppiano Licario*. México: Ediciones Era.

Lira Saade, Carmen. (2010). "Soy el responsable de la persecución a homosexuales que hubo en Cuba: Fidel Castro." *La Jornada*, August 31. Downloaded November 7, 2015. http://www.jornada.unam.mx/2010/08/31/index.php?article=026e1mun&section=mundo.

List Reyes, Mauricio. (2005). *Jóvenes corazones gay en la Ciudad de México*. Puebla: Universidad Autónoma de Puebla.

Long, Mary Kendall. (1995). *Salvador Novo: 1920–1940, between the Avant-Garde and the Nation*. Dissertation, Princeton University.

Long, William. (1994). "Lewd Painting of Revolutionary Draws Outrage in S. America: Some Intellectuals Warn that the Flap over the Portrait of Independence Leader Simon Bolivar May Fuel Censorship." *Los Angeles Times*, August 20. Downloaded December 16, 2015. http://articles.latimes.com/1994-08-20/news/mn-29159_1_simon-bolivar.

López, Miguel. (2014). *Un cuerpo ambulante: Sergio Zevallos en el grupo Chaclacayo (1982–1994)*. Trans. Max Hernández Calvo. Lima: Museo de Arte de Lima.

López, Miguel, and Giuseppe Campuzano. (2013). *The Museo Travesti del Perú and the Histories We Deserve*. Liverpool: Visible Works. Downloaded December 1, 2015. http://www.visibleproject.org/assets/medias/pdf/workbook02_Miguel%20Lopez.pdf.

Lossio, Julio. (2014–2015). "La dama de hierro: Luisa Revilla electa regidora del distrito de La Esperanza, Trujillo." *Crónicas de la diversidad*, 1:6, 4–6.

Lugones, María. (2007). "Heterosexualism and the Colonial/Modern Gender System." *Hypatia*, 22:1, 186–209.

Macías-González, Víctor. (2003). "The *Lagartijo* at *The High Life*: Masculine Consumption, Race, Nation, and Homosexuality in Porfirian Mexico." In Robert M. Irwin, Edward J. McCaughan, and Michelle Rocío Nasser, eds. *The Famous 41: Sexuality and Social Control in Mexico, 1901*. New York: Palgrave Macmillan, 227–249.

Magaña Moreno, Gandhi. (2016). "Las políticas de la Iglesia Católica hacia los homosexuales: El monstruo que hay que destruir." In Héctor Domínguez Ruvalcaba, ed. *La cuestión del odio: Acercamientos* *interdisciplinarios a la homofobia en México.*Xalapa: Universidad Veracruzana, 23–49.

Manrique, Jaime. (1999). *Eminent Maricones: Arenas, Lorca, Puig, and Me.* Madison: University of Wisconsin Press.

Marquet, Antonio. (2001). *¡Que se quede el infinito sin estrellas!*Mexico: Universidad Autónoma Metropolitana.

Martínez, Sanjuana. (2009). *Se venden niños.* Mexico: Editorial Planeta Mexicana.

Martínez-San Miguel, Yolanda. (2011). "'Sexilios': Hacia una nueva poética de la erótica caribeña." *América Latina Hoy,* 58, 15–30.

Mbembe, Achille. (2003). "Necropolitics." Trans. Libby Meintjes. *Public Culture,* 15:1, 11–40.

Meccia, Ernesto. (2011). *Los últimos homosexuales: Sociología de la homosexualidad y la gaycidad.* Buenos Aires: Gran Aldea Editores.

México, Iris. (2005). "Arte y símbolos patrios." *Escáner cultural* 7:71. Downloaded December 16, 2015. http://www.escaner.cl/escaner71/iris.html.

Miano Borruso, Marinella. (2003). *Hombres, mujeres y muxe' en el Istmo de Tehuantepec.* Mexico: Conaculta/INAH-Plaza y Valdés.

Mogrovejo, Norma. (2011). "Lo queer en América Latina: ¿Lucha identitaria, post-identitaria, asimilacionista o neocolonial?" In Daniel Balderston and Arturo Matute, eds. *Cartografías queer: Sexualidades y activismo LGBT en América Latina.* Pittsburgh: Instituto Internacional de Literatura Iberoamericana, 231–249.

— (2016). "Sexilio político." In Héctor Domínguez Ruvalcaba, ed. *La cuestión del odio: Acercamientos interdisciplinarios a la homofobia en México.*Xalapa: Universidad Veracruzana.

Molina, Fernando. (2015). "Evo Morales: 'No quiero pensar que usted es lesbiana.'" *El País,* November 17. Downloaded December 1, 2015. http://internacional.elpais.com/internacional/2015/11/17/actualidad/1447788400_619916.html.

Molloy, Sylvia. (1991). *At Face Value: Autobiography Writing in Spanish America.* Cambidge: Cambridge University Press.

— (2003). "Sentimental Excess and Gender Disruption: The Case of Amado Nervo." In Robert M. Irwin, Edward J. McCaughan, and Michelle Rocío Nasser, eds. *The Famous 41: Sexuality and Social Control in Mexico, 1901.* New York: Palgrave Macmillan, 291–306.

Monsiváis, Carlos. (1998). "Prólogo." In Salvador Novo, *La estatua de sal.* Mexico: CONACULTA, 13–72.

— (2001). "Una exposición, varias exposiciones, un tiempo de inauguraciones." In Círculo Cultural Gay, ed. *Una exposición, varias* *exposiciones, un tiempo de inauguraciones.*Mexico: Difusión Cultural UNAM-Museo Universitario del Chopo, 9–11.

— (2003). "The 41 and the *Gran Redada.*" In Robert M. Irwin, Edward J. McCaughan, and Michelle Rocío Nasser, eds. *The Famous 41: Sexuality and Social Control in Mexico, 1901.* New York: Palgrave Macmillan, 139–167.

Montecino, Sonia. (1996). *Madres y huachos: Alegorías del mestizaje chileno.* Santiago: Editorial Sudamericana.

Montero, Oscar. (1993). *Erotismo y representación en Julián del Casal.* Atlanta: Rodopi.

— (1998). "Modernismo y homofobia: Darío y Rodó." In Daniel Balderston and Donna J. Guy, eds. *Sexo y sexualidades en América Latina.* Buenos Aires: Paidós, 163–184.

Moraga, Cherríe. (1983). *This Bridge Called My Back: Writings by Radical Women of Color.*New York: Kitchen Table.

Morel, Blanca. (2007). "Nicaragua estrenará el 'más moderno' código penal." *El nuevo diario*, November 14. Downloaded July 20, 2016. http://www.elnuevodiario.com.ni/politica/2113-nicaragua-estrenara-mas-moderno-codigo-penal.

Muñoz, José Esteban. (1999). *Disidentifications: Queer of Color and the Performance of Politics.* Minneapolis: University of Minnesota Press.

— (2009). *Cruising Utopia: The Then and There of Queer Futurity.* New York: New York University Press.

Núñez Noriega, Guillermo. (2001). "Reconociendo los placeres, deconstruyendo las identidades: Antropología, patriarcado y homoerotismos en México." *Desacatos*, 6: 15–34.

— (1999 [1994]). *Sexo entre varones: Poder y resistencia en el campo sexual.* Mexico: Programa Universitario de Estudios de Género-Universidad Nacional Autónoma de México.

— (2005). "Significados y política de la 'diversidad sexual': ¿Sanización de la otredad o reivindicaciones de lo polimorfo? Reflexiones teóricas para el activismo." In Edith Yesenia Peña Sánchez, Francisco Ortiz Pedraza, and Lilia Hernádez Albarrán, eds. *Memorias de la II semana cultural de la diversidad sexual.* Mexico: Instituto Nacional de Antropología e Historia, 225–238.

— (2011). "Hombres indígenas, diversidad sexual y vulnerabilidad al VIH-SIDA: Una exploración sobre las dificultades académicas para estudiar un tema emergente en la antropología." *Desacatos*, 35, 13–28.

Ochoa, Marcia. (2014). *Queen for a Day:* Trasformistas*, Beauty Queens,* *and the Performance of Femininity in Venezuela.* Durham, NC: Duke University Press.

Ortiz, Fernando. (1973). *Contrapunteo cubano del tabaco y el azúcar.* Barcelona: Ariel.

Oyewumi, Oyeronke. (1997). *The Invention of Women: Making an African Sense of Western Gender Discourses.* Minneapolis: University of Minnesota Press.

Página Siete. (2015). "París el primer homosexual transformista en la política." May 31. Downloaded December 16, 2015. http://www. paginasiete.bo/nacional/2015/5/31/paris-primer-homosexual-transformista-politica-58395.html.

Parker, Richard. (1999). "'Within Four Walls': Brazilian Sexual Culture and HIV/AIDS." In Richard Parker and Peter Aggleton, ed. *Culture, Society, and Sexuality: A Reader.* London: Routledge, 253–266.

Parys, Jodie. (2012). *Writing AIDS: (Re)conceptualizing the Individual and Social Body in Spanish American Literature.* Columbus: Ohio State University Press.

Paz, Octavio. (1979). *El ogro filantrópico.* Barcelona: Seix Barral.

— (1987 [1974]). *Los hijos del limo.* Barcelona: Seix Barral.

— (2004 [1950]). *El laberinto de la soledad.* Mexico: Fondo de Cultura Económica.

Paz, Senel. (1990). *El bosque el lobo y el hombre nuevo.* La Habana: Ministerio de Cultura.

Perlongher, Néstor. (1987). *O negócio do Michê: A prostituição viril.* São Paulo: Editora Brasiliense.

Pierce, Joseph M. (2013). *Writing and Kinship in the Argentine fin de siglo, 1890–1910: La familia Bunge.* Dissertation, University of Texas.

Ponce, Patricia. (2001). "Sexualidades costeñas." *Desacatos,* 6, 111–136.

Prieur, Annick. (1998). *Mema's House: On Transvestites, Queens, and Machos.* Chicago: University of Chicago Press.

Puig, Manuel. (1976). *El beso de la mujer araña.* Barcelona: Seix Barral.

Quezada, Noemí. (1989). *Amor y magia amorosa entre los aztecas.* Mexico: UNAM.

Quijano, Aníbal. (2000). "Colonialidad del poder y clasificación social." *Journal of World-Systems Research,* 11:2, 342–386.

Quiroga, José. (1999). "Prólogo." In Daniel Balderston, *El deseo, enorme cicatriz luminosa.* Caracas: Ediciones eXcultura, 11–15.

— (2000). *Tropics of Desire: Interventions from Queer Latino America.* New York: New York University Press.

— (2010). "Prólogo." In José Quiroga, ed., *Mapa callejero: Crónicas sobre lo gay en América Latina*. Buenos Aires: Eterna Cadencia.

Rama, Ángel. (1998). *La ciudad letrada*. Montevideo: Arca.

Ramos, Samuel. (1982 [1934]). *El Perfil del hombre y la cultura en México*. México: Espasa Calpe.

Rancière, Jacques. (2010). *Dissensus: On Poticis and Aesthetics*. Trans. Steven Corcoran. New York: Continuum.

Revueltas, José. (1978). *Cuestionamientos e intenciones*. México: Era.

Reyes, Mario. (2005). "Unas vecinas muy peculiares … Las vecinas de la calle J." *Notiese: Salud, sexualidad y sida*, January 26. Downloaded December 18, 2015. http://www.notiese.org/notiese. php?ctn_id=957.

Reyes Ávila, Carlos. (2009). *Travesti*. México: Fondo Editorial Tierra Adentro.

Rivas San Martín, Felipe. (2012). "Gabriela Mistral: Lesbiana a toda prueba." *Columnas*, January. Downloaded June 9, 2015. http://columnasfeliperivas.blogspot.com/2012/01/gabriela-mistral-lesbiana-toda-prueba.html.

Rivera Cusicanqui, Silvia. (2010). *Violencias (re)encubiertas en Bolivia*. La Paz: Puerta Rota.

Rodgers, Mathew. (2013). "Brazil Has the Highest LGBT Murder Rate in the World." *FourTwoNine*, March. Downloaded October 16, 2015. http://dot429.com/articles/1641-brazil-retains-highest-lgbt-murder-rate-in-the-world.

Rodríguez Roch, Liana. (1997). "El sida en Cuba." *Papers*, 52, 177–186.

Rojas González, Francisco. (1984). *La negra Angustias*.México: Fondo de Cultura Económica.

Romero, Rubén José. (1964). *Apuntes de un lugareño*. In Antonio Castro Leal, ed. *La novela de la revolución mexicana*. Mexico: Aguilar, 51–139.

Salessi, Jorge. (1995). *Médicos, maleantes y maricas: Higiene, criminología y homosexualidad en la construcción de la nación argentina (Buenos Aires, 1871–1914)*. Rosario: Viterbo.

Sánchez Taylor, Jacqueline. (2000). "Tourism and 'Embodied' Commodities: Sex Tourism in the Caribbean." In Stephen Clift and Simon Carter, eds. *Tourism and Sex: Culture, Commerce and Coercion*. London: Pinter, 41–53.

Santiván, Fernando. (1955). *Memorias de un tolstoyano*, Santiago: Zig-zag.

Sarduy, Severo. (1982). *La simulación*. Caracas: Monte Ávila.

Scarry, Elaine. (1985). *The Body in Pain: The Making and Unmaking of the World*. New York: Oxford University Press.

Scheinman, Pamela. (2013). *Los Xitas de Corpus.* Mexico: Galería José María Velasco.

Schifter, Jacobo. (1999). *From Toads to Queens: Transvestism in a Latin American Setting.* New York: Harrington Park Press.

Sedgwick, Eve Kosowsky. (1990). *Epistemology of the Closet.* Berkeley: University of California Press.

Segato, Rita. (2011). "Género y decolonialidad: En busca de claves de lectura y de un vocabulario estratégico descolonial." In Karina Bidaseca and Vanesa Vázquez Laba, eds. *Feminismos y decolonialidad: Decolonizando el feminism desde y en América Latina.* Buenos Aires: Ediciones Godot, 17–48.

Sempol, Diego. (2013). *De los baños a la calle: Historia del movimiento lésbico, gay, trans uruguayo (1984–2013).* Montevideo: Random House Modadori and Ed. Sudamericana.

Sheridan, Guillermo. (1985). *Los contemporáneos ayer.* México: Fondo de Cultura Económica.

— (1999). *México en 1932: La polémica nacionalista.* Mexico: Fondo de Cultura Económica.

Sierra Madero, Abel. (2006). *Del otro lado del espejo: La sexualidad en la construcción de la nación cubana.* La Habana: Casa de las Américas.

Sifuentes-Jáuregui, Ben. (2002). *Transvestism, Masculinity, and Latin American Literature: Genders Share Flesh.* New York: Palgrave.

Sigal, Pete. (2007). "Queer Nahuatl: Sahagún's Faggots and Sodomites, Lesbians and Hermaphrodites." *Ethnohistory,* 54:1, 10–34.

Simon, Sherry. (1996). *Gender in Translation: Cultural Identity and the Politics of Transmission.* New York: Routledge.

Sívori, Horacio Federico. (2004). *Locas, chongos y gays: Sociabilidad homosexual masculina durante la década de 1990.* Buenos Aires: Antropogafia.

Sommer, Doris. (1991). *Foundational Fictions: The National Romances of Latin America.* Berkeley: University of California Press.

Spivak, Gayatri Chakravory. (2012). *An Aesthetic Education in the Era of Globalization.* Cambridge, MA: Harvard University Press.

Stryker, Susan. (2008). *Transgender History.* Berkeley: Seal Press.

Sutherland, Juan Pablo. (2001). "Introduction." In Juan Pablo Sutherland, ed. *A corazón abierto: Geografía literaria de la homosexualidad en Chile.* Santiago: Editorial Sudamericana, 9–31.

Taylor, Diana. (2003). *The Archive and the Repertoire: Performing Cultural Memories in the Americas.* Durham, NC: Duke University Press.

Télam. (2013). "México: Tras la aprobación del matromonio igualitario, aumenta la agresión a homosexuales." Downloaded October 18, 2015.

http://www.telam.com.ar/notas/201309/31836-mexico-tras-la-aprobacion-del-matrimonio-igualitario-aumenta-la-agresion-a-homosexuales.html.

Tortorici, Zeb. (2014). "Visceral Archives of the Body: Consuming the Dead, Digesting the Divine." *GLQ: A Journal of Lesbian and Gay Studies*, 20:4, 407–437.

Tzitsikos, Helene. (1985). *Fernando Santiván, humanista y literato.* Barcelona: Puvill Libros.

Valencia Triana, Sayak. (2010). *Capitalismo gore.* Barcelona: Melusina.

Vargas, Javi. (2014). "Pedro Palanca: La errancia de torcidos pies." *Crónicas de la diversidad*, August–September, 8–9.

Vasconcelos, José. (1929). *La raza cósmica: Misión de la raza iberoamericana.* Paris: Agencia Mundial de Librería.

Villanueva-Collado, Alfredo. (1996). "El puer virginal y el doble: Configuraciones arquetípicas en la pasión y muerte del cura Deusto, por Augusto d'Hlamar." *Chasqui: Revista de Literatura Latinoamericana*, 25:1, 3–11.

Wolf, Sherry. (2009). *Sexuality and Socialism: History, Politics, and Theory of LGBT Liberation.* Chicago: Haymarket.

Zaid, Gabriel. (2015). "Las bodas." *Letras Libres*, October. Downloaded November 18, 2015. http://www.letraslibres.com/blogs/articulos-recientes/las-bodas.

Zapata, Luis. (1979). *El vampiro de la Colonia Roma.* Mexico: Grijalbo.

Index

Note: Page numbers followed by *n* indicate a footnote.